# THE DTI EURO MANUAL
*Linking EC legislation to UK business functions*

# The
# DTI
## Euro Manual

*Linking EC legislation to UK business functions*

## Volume I
*How business functions are affected*

the department for Enterprise

## CCH Editions Limited
TAX, BUSINESS AND LAW PUBLISHERS

Published by CCH Editions Limited
Telford Road, Bicester, Oxfordshire OX6 0XD
Tel. (0869) 253300. Facsimile (0869) 245814.
DX: 83750 Bicester 2.

| | |
|---|---|
| EUROPE | CCH Europe Inc., Wiesbaden, Germany. |
| USA | Commerce Clearing House, Inc., Chicago, Illinois. |
| CANADA | CCH Canadian Limited, Toronto, Ontario. |
| AUSTRALIA | CCH Australia Limited, North Ryde, NSW. |
| NEW ZEALAND | CCH New Zealand Limited, Auckland. |
| SINGAPORE | CCH Asia Limited. |
| JAPAN | CCH Japan Limited, Tokyo. |

This publication is sold with the understanding that no legal or other professional services are being rendered. If legal advice or other expert assistance is required, the services of a competent professional person should be sought.

Ownership of Trade Marks

The Trade Marks

CCH ACCESS, COMPUTAX and **COMMERCE CLEARING HOUSE, INC.** are the property of Commerce Clearing House, Incorporated, Chicago, Illinois, USA

**British Library Cataloguing in Publication Data.**

Department of Trade & Industry
  DTI Euro Manual: Linking EC Law to UK
  Business Functions
  I. Title
  344.10665

  ISBN 0–86325–309–1 (Both volumes)
       0–86325–307–5 (Volume 1)
       0–86325–308–3 (Volume 2)

© Copyright Controller HMSO 1993

All rights reserved. No part of this work covered by the publisher's copyright may be reproduced or copied in any form or by any means (graphic, electronic or mechanical, including photocopying, recording, recording taping, or information and retrieval systems) without the written permission of the publisher.

Typeset in Great Britain by Mendip Communications Ltd, Frome.
Printed and bound in Great Britain by The Eastern Press Ltd, Reading.

# Preface by the President of the Board of Trade

1 January 1993 marked the official opening of the single market: the formal date when the home market for UK business enlarged from 55 million customers to 340 million.

There is now very widespread awareness of the importance of this enlarged market in the minds of the men and women who manage and work in our companies.

It is equally self-evident that many of our companies have made significant inroads into that market place, proving both the will to do so and the ability to compete. In 1991, 57 per cent of UK trade was with the EC, compared to 43 per cent in 1981.

The changes which have taken place as a result of the single market are having significant effects on companies. For example, routine customs clearance of commercial goods and 60 million customs forms have now been abolished. For manufacturers of many products, instead of different standards in each member state, many products now normally only need to be certified once to be marketable in all member states. There are many other examples one could take, but of particular importance is the opening of public contracts to Europe-wide bidding. Public purchasing comprises around 15 per cent of Community gross domestic product. That market alone is worth £318bn a year and, without doubt, the construction industries of all the Community countries will be in there fighting for their share.

On 25 January 1993, I launched the 'Business in Europe' service. It is targeted at the business community. It pulls together work on promoting the single market with the hitherto separate provision of export services to the European market. It enables several new Department of Trade and Industry services to be focused on our most important market, and provides practical help and advice on most problems to be faced when doing business in Europe. Other initiatives are also being pushed forward, including examining ways in which to reduce the administrative burden on business. Also, we are energetically pursuing measures to ensure that the single market works, and that there is a level playing field across Europe.

This book is part of 'Business in Europe'. It summarises the framework of EC legislation within which Community businesses must work. It covers various legal issues but it is not a legal text book. It is written for the business reader and so legal issues are dealt with in broad outline. It summarises UK implementation and points to how to find out about implementation in other Community countries. Its particular strength is that it links EC legislation to business function to enable managers, whether the sales director of a large PLC or production manager of a small firm, to identify the areas where action should be taken.

The DTI Euro Manual is required reading for all who are determined to help their businesses respond to the opportunities of Europe.

The Right Honourable Michael Heseltine MP,<br>
President of the Board of Trade<br>
London<br>
February 1993.

# Introduction

The creation of the single market is the major development of the European Community in recent times, and is one in which the UK has taken a major part: it was the brainchild of the UK Commissioner, Lord Cockfield, and was finalised during the UK Presidency of the EC in the second half of 1992.

In order to lay a firm foundation for the single market, and to ensure that the European market is truly open, over 500 measures have been adopted by the EC in the seven years to the end of 1992: the original target was 282. These measures have, among other things, removed physical barriers to the transport of most goods, put European standards and arrangements for testing and certification in place and put public procurement on a Community-wide basis. Obviously, further measures will be needed to fine tune the operation of the single market, but the framework we have now will enable business people to identify and respond to the potential for their products in today's climate. It will also enable them to make sound decisions, knowing that all firms in the EC are under the same broad obligations.

Those changes affect every aspect of running a business from the use of VDUs to the disposal of waste and from the protection of pregnant workers to the publication of accounts. All business people have to be aware of those developments and their implications for their firms. In doing so, they will enable themselves to tap into the new home market of over 340 million customers, and to get into the rest of Europe the way the rest of Europe will inevitably want to get into the UK.

Through its 'Europe Open for Business' campaign, the Department of Trade and Industry has given business people in the UK the information they need to keep pace with the single market programme. While surveys show that most medium-sized and larger firms have taken action to prepare for the single market, many, particularly smaller businesses who do not export, still believe that the single market does not affect them. However, whether a company is well prepared or only just getting to grips with the changes, it needs to understand the measures and be sure of their impact on its business. To help in this, the *DTI Euro Manual* provides businesses with an extensive summary of EC measures affecting business. The Manual includes developments up to 31 December 1992 and covers implementation of legislation in the UK, and how to find out about implementation in other member states. It has been prepared with the business reader in mind, dealing with the various legal issues in broad outline, but the manual should not be used as an alternative to obtaining legal advice. Although it is not a legal text book, accountants, lawyers and other business advisers such as trade associations, Chambers of Commerce and consultants will find it to be a useful source of reference.

The Euro Manual's particular strength, and what sets it apart from other books on the subject, is that it links EC measures to particular business functions to enable managers – whether the marketing director of a public limited company or the personnel manager of a small firm – to identify areas which need action. Since it concentrates on measures which affect any UK business, trading in Europe or not, the Euro Manual is a vital asset for all those who are determined to help their businesses make the most of the single market.

# How to use the DTI Euro Manual

The DTI Euro Manual is divided into two volumes. Volume 1 contains general descriptions of how and why EC measures affect business on a function-by-function basis. Volume 2 contains more information on specific measures and proposals. These are divided up according to areas of policy.

To access the information contained in the Manual you should:

- Turn to the chapter in Volume 1 which deals with your business responsibilities (for example, purchasing, Chapter 2),
- Go to the section of that chapter which covers the policy area with which you are concerned (for example, public procurement, section 2.6).
- The questions you will find there will confirm whether or not you are affected and briefly discuss why and how this is so.
- You will then be referred onto Volume 2, where you will find more detailed information, and to the Know-How Appendix for sources of further help.

The matrix on the next page will allow you quicker access to the topics in Volume 2. The index at the end of Volume 2 will direct you straight to specific subjects in both volumes.

In order to distinguish between those measures which are already, or are about to be, in force and proposals, which are not in force and are still subject to change, the proposals are in *italic* type.

# Quick-access Matrix

References are to page numbers in Volume 1

| | Sales and Marketing | Purchasing | Operations and logistics | Human resources | Information systems | Research and product development | Finance | Corporate affairs |
|---|---|---|---|---|---|---|---|---|
| Free movement of goods, people, services and capital | 3 | | | | | | 137 | 157 |
| Standards | 4 | | 79 | | | 123 | | 159 |
| Transport | 7 | 49 | 77 | | | | | |
| VAT | 9 | | | | | | 138 | |
| Excise duties | 11 | 53 | 81 | | | | | |
| Frontier controls | 14 | 55 | 83 | | | | | |
| Trade policy and customs duties | 15 | 56 | 84 | | | | | 161 |
| Freedom of movement for workers | 17 | 58 | 85 | 105 | | | | |
| Employment | | | 87 | 107 | | | | 162 |
| Health and safety | | | 89 | 111 | | | | |
| Public procurement | 18 | 59 | | | | | | 163 |
| Energy | 21 | 62 | 93 | | | | | |
| Environmental policy | 23 | 64 | 94 | | | 125 | 141 | 166 |
| Consumer protection | 24 | | | | | | | 167 |
| Intellectual property | 27 | | | | 117 | 126 | 142 | 169 |
| Information technologies and telecommunications | 30 | 65 | | | 119 | 127 | | |
| Company law | 33 | | | 113 | | 129 | 143 | 172 |
| Company taxation | | | | | | | 145 | |
| Financial services | 34 | 67 | | | | | 147 | 175 |
| Insurance | 36 | 69 | | | | | 149 | |
| State aids | 38 | | | | | | | 177 |
| Structural funds | 39 | | | 115 | | | 153 | 178 |
| Competition policy | 40 | | 96 | | | | | 179 |
| Food law | 42 | 71 | 98 | | | 130 | | |
| Pharmaceuticals | 44 | 73 | 100 | | | 132 | 151 | 182 |
| Animal, plant and fish health and hygiene | | | | | | | | |

# Definition of the business functions used in this book

Below is short description of the scope of each business function.

**Sales and Marketing**  The legislation relevant to these two functions is similar and in many small firms the functions are combined. For these reasons they are treated together.

**Purchasing**  This covers all procurement of goods and services.

**Operations and Logistics**  This covers health and safety and other employment issues, as well as those involving the environment. Also included are delivery and distribution of raw materials and finished products.

**Human resources**  This term covers all aspects of recruiting, managing, training and compensating a firm's employees.

**Information systems**  This function covers information systems in its broadest sense and is not limited to electronic data processing.

**Research and product development**  The coverage of the product development function includes intellectual property rights (IPR).

**Finance**  Includes financial and management accounting and treasury.

**Corporate Affairs**  This covers areas such as company law, compliance and corporate PR issues.

# Acknowledgements

The DTI would like to thank Ernst and Young Management Consultants, who prepared the first draft for the DTI and the liaison group of business support organisations who gave advice to help ensure that the book meets the needs of business.

The DTI would also like to thank the officials across Whitehall departments who contributed to this manual. In particular the Ministry for Agriculture, Fisheries and Food, the Health and Safety Executive, HM Treasury, the Employment Department Group, the Department of Environment, the Department of Transport, HM Customs and Excise, the Central Statistical Office, the Home Office, the Department of Health, the Department of National Heritage, the Inland Revenue and, of course, the officials within the DTI.

# Contents

Preface by the President of the Board of Trade    v
Introduction    vii
How to Use the DTI Euro Manual    ix
Quick-access Matrix    x
Definition of Business Functions used in this book    xi
Acknowledgements    xii

1  The Sales and Marketing function    1
2  The Purchasing function    47
3  The Operations and Logistics function    75
4  The Human Resources function    103
5  The Information Systems function    115
6  The Research and Product Development function    121
7  The Finance function    135
8  The Corporate Affairs function    155
   Appendixes
   I  The Know-How Appendix    183
   II  The European Economic Area    211

# 1 · The **SALES AND MARKETING** function

| | | |
|---|---|---|
| 1.1 | Free movement of goods, people, services and capital | 3 |
| 1.2 | Standards | 4 |
| 1.3 | Transport | 7 |
| 1.4 | VAT | 9 |
| 1.5 | Excise duties | 11 |
| 1.6 | Frontier controls | 14 |
| 1.7 | Trade policy and customs duties | 15 |
| 1.8 | Freedom of movement for workers | 17 |
| 1.9 | Public procurement | 18 |
| 1.10 | Energy | 21 |
| 1.11 | Environmental policy | 23 |
| 1.12 | Consumer protection | 24 |
| 1.13 | Intellectual property | 27 |
| 1.14 | Information technologies and telecommunications | 30 |
| 1.15 | Company law | 33 |
| 1.16 | Financial services | 34 |
| 1.17 | Insurance | 36 |
| 1.18 | State aids | 38 |

| | | |
|---|---|---|
| **1.19** | **Structural funds** | 39 |
| **1.20** | **Competition policy** | 40 |
| **1.21** | **Food law** | 42 |
| **1.22** | **Pharmaceuticals** | 44 |

# 1.1 Free movement of goods, people, services and capital

## Are you affected?
Your business is affected if:
- you sell goods to or services in other member states.

## Why?
In order to eliminate all obstacles to the free movement of goods, the Community has established the rule that member states should not maintain or erect barriers to intra-community trade. This principle is set out in Articles (Arts.) 30 and 34 of the Treaty of Rome.

To eliminate obstacles to the free movement of services, the Community established, in Art. 59 of the Treaty of Rome the right for suppliers of services, regardless of where they are based within the Community, to carry on their business anywhere in the Community under the same conditions as local competitors. In addition, Art. 52 ensures the principle of freedom of establishment for companies or firms, under the conditions laid down for its own nationals by the law of the country where these companies or firms establish themselves.

The provisions of Arts. 30, 34, 52 and 59 should make it easier for you to provide services in other member states under the same conditions as their nationals. These provisions also facilitate trade with other member states.

## How?
Articles 30 and 34 of the Treaty established the principles that member states cannot introduce or maintain quantitative restrictions (or measures which have an equivalent effect) on imports from and exports to other member states. Article 59 established the right for a business in one member state to provide services in the other member states.

Rules on the free movement of goods and services in the Community enable you to offer your products or services on a Community-wide basis. The principle of freedom of establishment also ensures the right for businesses to set up an agency, branch or subsidiary anywhere in the Community. This makes operating throughout the Community much easier and expansion into new markets more feasible. However, free movement of goods and services is also likely to lead to increased competition on your current markets.

## Further information
Turn to the Free Movement of goods, people, services and capital topic at p. 1 in Volume 2 for more detailed coverage of these Articles.

# 1.2 Standards

## Are you affected?

Your business is affected if:

- your products conform to a national or European standard;
- as a provider of goods or services, your processes or systems could be considered to be of a high standard.

## Why?

- If your product is covered by one of the Community's technical standards Directives, whether it is an 'old' or a New Approach measure, it must conform to the technical details or essential requirements as outlined in the Directive so that it can be sold in the EC. This applies whether or not the product is traded across borders.

  Products which conform to esssential requirements of New Approach Directives must be 'CE' marked. The marking is an indication to national enforcement bodies – for example, trading standards departments or the Health and Safety Executive in the UK – that your product complies with the 'essential requirements' of the Directives for which it is affixed.

  The Community is trying to prevent the establishment of new technical regulations which could constitute barriers to trade within the Community. Member states are required to notify the Commission in draft of any new technical regulations relating to any industrial or agricultural product. Other member states may then object on the grounds that they constitute technical barriers to trade.

- BS 5750 is a standard recognising quality management systems or processes, and is identical to the international ISO9000 standard and European standard EN29000. Attaining BS 5750 creates confidence with customers that your product will conform consistently to a standard or specification.

## How?

The main ways in which the sales and marketing function may be affected by EC standards measures are:

### Removal of barriers to trade

The main issues for your function regarding standards are those of free circulation and the removal of the need for added local or national compliance.

A number of products fall within the New Approach Directives, which outline the essential requirements which the product must meet. These essential requirements are underpinned by national standards implementing specified European standards. The easiest way to ensure your product conforms to the relevant Directive is to ensure that it complies with national standards. If it does, no member state can refuse to allow your products on the market on technical grounds (except where standards are subsequently found to be deficient).

Where no European legislation exists, the general principle is that if a product is fit to be sold in one member state, it is fit to be sold in any other – there is mutual recognition by member states of each other's national regulations pending the development of measures underpinning 'essential requirements'. However, there can still be national objections to selling the product in that country on the grounds of health, safety or environmental impact.

## Conforming to technical requirements

It is very important that you clarify whether your product is covered by an old or New Approach Directive, and that, if it is, it conforms to that Directive. If, for any reason, your product does not conform to the technical details or essential requirements outlined in the Directive, you will not be allowed to sell it anywhere in the Community, regardless of whether or not it is traded across frontiers. The easiest way of ensuring that your product meets the requirements of a New Approach Directive is to ensure that it conforms to the national standard implementing a specified European standard. New Approach Directives are underpinned by European standards prepared by European standards bodies, usually CEN or CENELEC. They are then implemented as identically worded national standards.

## New standards as barriers to trade

New Approach Directives only outline the essential requirements that a product must meet in order to be sold in the Community. Although, under Community law, member state authorities are required to accept products on their market which conform to the legislation and standards of other member states where these are intended to achieve equivalent objectives, the same principle of 'mutual recognition' cannot be applied to the individual purchaser in the market who is free to set his own requirements, often by reference to national standards (not implementing European standards).

There are a number of ways in which you can keep abreast of developments. The DTI circulates details of notification of draft new technical regulations to those most likely to be affected, and brief details are published weekly by the Association of British Chambers of Commerce in 'Business Briefing'. They are also available on Spearhead, the DTI's single market database.

## CE marking – proposed reconciliation of Directives

In the current proposal, if your product conforms to essential requirements, it must be CE marked. You may also have to affix the identification number of the organisation which tested or certified your product. Finally, other marks which you may currently use may be affected by the proposal. You may, therefore, wish to monitor the outcome of the proposal to ensure that you comply, and that any sales or marketing strategies which involve existing marks are not affected.

### BS 5750

BS 5750 lists the key requirements of a quality management system, which can be applied to almost any type of organisation. It is identical to the international ISO9000 standard and the European EN29000 standard. They include the need to establish a quality policy, to allocate responsibility clearly, to give authority to those allocated responsibility, to document each stage of the production process, and to establish systems for identifying, remedying and preventing defects in quality.

## Further information

Turn to the Standards topic at p. 13 in Volume 2 for more detailed coverage of these measures and proposed measures.

# 1.3 Transport

## Are you affected?
Your business is affected if:
- you make use of freight transport services;
- you sell to providers of freight transport services.

## Why?
- Likely reductions in transport costs and times as a result of the liberalisation of Community freight transport may enable you to expand your market to include other member states. At the same time, you may face increasing competition as member state competitors take advantage of these improvements and enter your domestic market.
- The overall objective of Community legislation is to allow all member state providers of freight transport to offer their services throughout the EC. Since you sell to this type of customer, you should have a wider choice of customers as the industry undergoes major restructuring and more transport firms enter the UK market. In addition, your current customer base may decide to extend their scope of operations to include other member state markets. The kinds of services you offer and their scope may need to change in order to meet the changes in customers' needs.

## How?
The Community has adopted a number of measures enabling companies to offer transport services freely throughout the Community. This liberalisation is likely to lead to:
- increased competition in all transport sectors;
- a downward pressure on margins; and
- some industry restructuring, with a potential increase of concentration within the UK industry.

It is likely that your own access to Community markets will improve as operators offer more competitive transport services. At the same time, these improvements should facilitate access to your domestic market for non-UK competitors, so there may be a need to defend your current customer base.

Changes are likely to be greater for cross-frontier transport rather than internal UK services, as the UK already has a largely deregulated system.

Those who sell to transport firms may benefit from evaluating:
- their ability to respond effectively to these changes in transport customers' industries;

# 8 · THE **SALES AND MARKETING** FUNCTION

- if appropriate, their ability to serve new customers in both the UK and other member states.

## Further information

Turn to the Transport topic at p. 27 in Volume 2 for more detailed coverage of these measures.

# 1.4 VAT

## Are you affected?

Your business is affected if:

- your business is VAT-registered;
- you sell goods and services liable for VAT to other member states;
- you intend to sell goods and services liable for VAT to other member states;
- you are involved in distance selling, such as mail order.

## Why?

VAT was one of the most contentious issues within the single market programme. Recently, agreement was reached on the VAT rates Directive (No. 92/77/EEC) establishing a time-limited minimum standard rate of VAT, and one or two optional reduced rates which may be applied to an agreed list of goods and services. Agreement was also reached on the administration of VAT after the abolition of frontier VAT controls.

The sales and marketing function should be aware of the long term implications of the following:

- the abolition of VAT controls at frontiers for EC goods;
- new rules on distance sales, including mail order.

## How?

The main ways in which the sales and marketing function may be affected by EC VAT measures are:

### The destination principle

From 1 January 1993 to at least the end of 1996, most cross-border commercial VAT transactions continue to be based on the destination principle. This means that intra-Community sales continue to be zero-rated by the seller, and VAT is paid by the VAT-registered customer at the rate in force in the country of consumption. The abolition of VAT controls at frontiers prevents delays caused by goods being held at borders prior to payment of VAT.

### Changes in rates

Some member states had to raise the level of VAT on certain products to bring them near to, or in line with, the agreed minimum standard rate of 15 per cent, and this may reduce demand. The abolition of frontier controls leaves consumers free to shop cross-border with certain exceptions such as new motorised land vehicles, boats and aircraft, and to take advantage of lower tax rates in neighbouring member states. This may also affect regional sales for some products, depending on differences in national VAT rates and access to products.

The effect on demand may be even more pronounced if goods are also subject to excise duties.

### Cross-border mail order

Detailed rules for the management of VAT on cross-border mail order transactions have been set down, which mean that sellers will have to set up a taxable presence in the relevant market if their sales in that member state exceed ECU 100,000 per annum. Member states can also opt for a lower threshold of ECU 35,000. This gives mail order businesses the tax framework within which to develop their business in other member states.

## Further information

Turn to the VAT topic at p. 47 in Volume 2 for more detailed coverage of these measures and proposals.

# 1.5 Excise duties

## Are you affected?

Your business is affected if:

- you sell tobacco in the UK or other Community countries;
- you sell spirits, wines, beers, cider or perry in the UK or other Community countries;
- any of your sales are duty free;
- you retail fuel oils in the UK or other Community countries.

## Why?

- The Agreement to impose a harmonised structure and minimum rate of excise duty on cigarettes and other tobacco products required some member states to impose higher duties on these products than previously.
- The Agreement to impose a harmonised structure and minimum rates of excise duty on spirits, wine, beer, cider, perry and intermediate products required some member states to raise their duties.
- The eventual abolition of intra-Community duty-free sales in 1999 will affect retailers offering such sales. Vendor control of sales of duty-free products until 1999 places additional responsibility on the retailer.
- The harmonisation of the structure of duties and minimum rates on mineral oils may have an impact on prices across the Community.

## How?

The main ways in which the sales and marketing function are affected by EC excise duties policy are:

### Cigarettes

The agreement for a minimum rate of 57 per cent of the retail price (including tax) in the most popular price category per 1,000 cigarettes means increases in the cost of cigarettes in some member states. This agreement could result in reduced demand or increased costs for companies if they choose to absorb some of the extra cost of the duty. Spain, Italy, Greece and France needed to increase their rates of tax (duty and VAT) on cigarettes to meet the agreed minimum rate.

### Beer

Luxembourg, France, Spain and Portugal needed to increase their excise duty to meet the agreed minimum of ECU 1.87 for every degree of alcohol per 100 litres. This could result in reduced demand in these markets or increased costs if companies choose to absorb some of the extra cost of the duty.

### Cider and perry

The agreement classified cider and perry as 'other fermented beverages' (not beer or wine) which may be liable to a reduced duty rate. This allowed the UK to retain its existing duty structure on these products.

### Spirits

A minimum rate of ECU 550 per hectolitre of pure alcohol (hlpa) was agreed for spirits. However, member states who previously applied a rate not exceeding ECU 1,000 per hlpa may not reduce it. In addition, member states who previously applied a rate in excess of ECU 1,000 per hlpa may not reduce it below ECU 1,000. The agreement did not require any member state to increase its duty on spirits.

### Still and sparkling wine

A minimum rate of zero was agreed for wines. Sales in high-duty states could be affected by cross-border shopping, as consumers take advantage of the abolition of frontier controls to purchase cheaper goods.

### Intermediate products

A minimum duty rate for intermediate products (fortified beverages such as vermouth) of ECU 45 per hectolitre of product was agreed. This required Portugal to raise its excise duty on these products.

### Duty-free sales

The original proposal to abolish duty-free sales with frontier controls on 1 January 1993 was changed. Existing intra-Community 'duty-free' sales arrangements will remain until 1 July 1999. Duty-free sales for travellers departing for countries outside the Community will continue after 1999. Following the removal of fiscal frontiers, a system of vendor control of duty-free sales has been introduced.

### Mineral oils

- *Diesel*: the agreed minimum rate of excise on diesel could lead to an alteration of relative pricing within the Community.
- *Heating fuels*: the minimum duty for heating gas oil was set at ECU 18 per 1,000 litres. However, those member states who, on 1 January 1991, applied a zero rate may continue to do so provided they apply a control levy of ECU 5 per 1,000 litres from 1 January 1993. The charge may be increased to ECU 10 per 1,000 litres on 1 January 1995, if problems of trade distortion are identified. The minimum rate for kerosene used for heating purposes was set at zero.

- *Leaded and unleaded petrol*: the minimum excise rate for unleaded petrol was set ECU 50 below that of leaded (respectively ECU 287 and ECU 337 per 1,000 litres). These rates are below the current UK rate, so no change to the UK rate was required as a result of this agreement.

## Further information

Turn to the Excise duties topic at p. 63 in Volume 2 for more detailed coverage of these measures and proposals.

# 1.6 Frontier controls

## Are you affected?
Your business is affected if:
- you sell products in the UK or in any other member state.

## Why?
The future ability of Community businesses to offer their products on a Community-wide basis should now be enhanced by the abolition of border controls on the distribution of goods between member states since 1 January 1993. As transport times and costs reduce as a result, businesses may be able to reduce the lead times needed to meet cross-border transactions, and allow them to consider supplying geographically more distant customers within the Community.

## How?
The main way in which the sales and marketing function is affected by EC frontier controls measures is:

### Reduced costs and transportation times
The overall objective of the Community's frontier controls legislation is to abolish restrictions on the free movement of goods between member states. To facilitate this, the Community drew up a two-stage system, the first stage being effective from 1 January 1988.

The key element of the first stage was that all member states would recognise a single administrative document (SAD) for customs clearance purposes. This simplified the paperwork involved in transporting goods between member states. Previously, as many as 70 different forms needed to be completed.

Stage two involved the co-ordination of policies and the adoption of common legislation to allow the elimination of internal frontiers and controls on the movement of goods within the EC, including the SAD, by 1993.

These initiatives, combined with the improvements under way in the Community's transport industries, are likely to lead to transport costs being reduced by up to 5 per cent and transport times being reduced by up to 30 per cent, depending on the routes taken.

## Further information
Turn to the Frontier controls topic at p. 69 in Volume 2 for more detailed coverage of these measures.

# 1.7 Trade policy and customs duties

## Are you affected?

Your business is affected if:

- you import goods from countries outside the Community for re-sale in the UK, other member states or European Free Trade Association (EFTA) countries;
- you import or export goods between the Community and members of EFTA.

## Why?

The disappearance of frontier controls will signal the end of national quantitative restrictions. Instead, a considerably more liberal Community input regime is under discussion. This is likely to include only a limited number of quotas applied on a Community-wide basis.

Article 115 of the Treaty of Rome has afforded individual member states the ability, where justified, and where the European Commission agrees, to restrict the import of non-Community goods in free circulation in the rest of the Community. With the disappearance of frontier controls between member states on 1 January 1993, the restrictions contained in Art. 115 are expected to play a much-reduced role.

## How?

The main ways in which the sales and marketing function will be affected by EC trade and customs duties policy are:

### The EEA agreement

The formation of the European Economic Area (EEA) may make markets within the EFTA countries more attractive to you. Although border formalities will remain, many of the non-tariff barriers to trade will be removed making it easier to trade in EFTA markets.

### Rules of origin

Rules of origin are used to establish the country of origin of goods for purposes of international trade. They are particularly important where products have undergone processing in several countries. If you trade with EFTA countries, you may benefit from the simplification of these rules under the EEA agreement.

### Community quotas

Each member state has, for many years, applied a variety of differing national quantitative restrictions. Such restrictions are, however, inconsistent with the completion of the single market. A Community-wide quota regime is therefore under discussion between the European Commission and the member states. It is not yet clear exactly what the scope of the new regime will be or how it will operate, but economic justification will be a prime consideration in deciding which quotas should be put on a Community footing. Most existing quotas applied throughout the Community will be abolished. The only exceptional cases where member states may possibly maintain national quotas during the initial months of 1993 pending the establishment of a Community-wide regime are likely to be bananas originating from 'dollar' countries and certain steel products.

### Article 115 restrictions

These are special restrictions on imports which (if allowed to do so by the European Commission) individual member states may apply to products originating from outside the Community but in free circulation within it. With the disappearance of internal frontiers and the associated border controls and checks on trade between the Community member states, and the establishment of a Community-wide quota regime, it is much less likely that occasions will arise where Art. 115 restrictions are appropriate. Therefore, Art. 115 is expected to play only a limited role in the future trade policy of individual member states. Normally, you should be free to re-export goods to other Community markets without restriction.

## Further information

Turn to the Trade policy and customs duty topic at p. 79 in Volume 2 for more detailed coverage of these measures and proposals and how far they are extended to the EFTA countries.

# 1.8 Freedom of movement for workers

## Are you affected?

Your business is affected if:

- you provide professional services in more than one member state.

## Why?

In order to complete the single market and, in particular, to eliminate remaining obstacles to the freedom of movement for workers, the Community is seeking to ensure the recognition of professional qualifications, that is, the right for fully qualified professionals from one member state to join their profession and practise in another member state.

## How?

The main way in which the sales and marketing function will be affected by the freedom of movement for workers is:

### Professional services

The first general Directive on higher education diplomas sets out a system for 'mutual recognition' of professional qualifications which require at least three years' degree-level study. It applies to professions which are regulated directly or indirectly by the state including professions regulated by chartered bodies.

This should make it easier for you to be authorised by corresponding professional bodies in other member states in order to provide services there from a UK base or to set up practices there. However, this will also mean greater competition in the UK market, because professionals from other member states will be able to gain authorisation from professional bodies in the UK in order to set up businesses here and provide services to UK customers.

## Further information

Turn to the Freedom of movement for workers topic at p. 89 in Volume 2 for more detailed coverage of this measure.

# 1.9 Public procurement

## Are you affected?

Your business is affected if:

- you do or could sell to local or central government, or to public bodies such as health authorities or police forces;
- you do or could sell to utilities which operate water, electricity, gas, telecommunications or transport networks providing services to the public;
- you sell to the oil and coal extraction industries, in particular, private sector organisations which have exclusive rights to exploit a geographical area to explore for, or extract, oil, gas or solid fuel;
- you sell to ports or airports, in particular, private sector organisations which enjoy exclusive rights to provide terminal facilities for transport carriers by air, sea or inland waterway.

## Why?

Until recently, the vast majority of public sector (such as government) contracts in the Community are awarded to local or national contractors, and only a tiny fraction to firms from other member states. The public procurement rules (in most cases) prohibit public purchasers from favouring local or national suppliers, by requiring and enforcing fully competitive tendering procedures. From 1993, the procurement rules also apply to private sector bodies in the energy, water, transport and telecommunications sectors.

The public procurement rules therefore have a significant impact on selling to the European public sector and utilities market. They open up new markets, increase competition in existing markets, and often require changes to methods of selling.

## How?

The main ways in which the sales and marketing function will be affected by the EC public procurement rules are:

### Customers

If you have any of the following kinds of customers, they have to comply with the public procurement rules:

- central, regional and/or local government;
- other public bodies such as health services and police forces;
- any public organisation coming within the GATT agreement on government procurement (GPA);

# PUBLIC PROCUREMENT · 19

- utilities, both publicly and privately owned.

The public procurement rules open up potential new markets (for example, in other member states) and your existing markets may also be increasingly open to your competitors. Many of these types of customers have to publish an advance indication of their annual purchasing requirements.

## Products and services

These products and services are covered by the public procurement rules:

- building and civil engineering works;
- supplies of goods on purchase or hire;
- a wide range of services such as consultancy and computer services, accounting, cleaning, property maintenance and refuse disposal from 1 July 1993.

Contracts below the following thresholds are not covered:

- *Supplies and services:*
  regional and local government: approx. £140,000;
  central Government and other bodies covered by GPA; approx. £88,800;
- *Building works including work divided into lots:* approx. £3.5m;
- *Utilities*
  supplies to the telecommunications sector: approx. £420,000;
  supplies to other sectors: approx. £280,000;
  building works: approx. £3.5m.

The following hierarchy of standards must be used in the public sector:

- national standards implementing European standards;
- national standards implementing international standards;
- national standards;
- any other standards.

The utilities must use:

- national standards implementing European standards;
- other recognised standards.

## Selling

How you sell your products or services will be affected by a number of procedures which organisations must use when purchasing:

- *advertising rules*: in the public sector, all tenders above the financial threshold must be advertised in the *Official Journal of the European Communities*. This information is also available on Tenders Electronic Daily. In the utilities sector, purchasers may advertise qualification systems, or invite interest in periodic indicative notices;

- *tendering procedures*: purchasers may use open, restricted or (in the utilities sector and in exceptional cases in the public sector) negotiated procedures;
- *qualifications*: suppliers may be asked to meet conditions laid down by the purchaser by giving evidence of their business, financial or technical position;
- *award criteria*: the criteria are either price alone, or a combination of factors which makes the tender the 'most economically advantageous'. These might include, for example, price, quality and delivery. Purchasers must say in advance what the criteria will be, and must abide by them when assessing bids;
- *time limits*: the minimum time between first advertising a tender and the closing date is specified, and can vary between 37 and 52 days, depending on which procedure is used. In certain circumstances, necessitating urgency, these can be reduced to 10 days respectively.

## Compliance

The compliance Directives ensure that firms who think they have been harmed by a breach of the rules will have the same level of legal protection in all member states. In the UK, redress will be through the courts.

# Further information

Turn to the Public procurement topic at p. 153 in Volume 2 for more detailed coverage of these measures.

# 1.10 Energy

## Are you affected?

Your business is affected if:

- you are an energy supplier or are otherwise involved in the supply of energy;
- you supply products (or components of products) which are significant users of energy.

## Why?

- The Community is attempting to create the conditions for an internal energy market. This will make it easier for utilities in one member state to buy gas and electricity from another.
- The Community is also attempting to increase energy efficiency. This will lead to increased energy labelling requirements, and the introduction of more technical standards for energy-using equipment such as boilers.

## How?

The main ways in which the sales and marketing function will be affected are:

### Transit of electricity and gas

The European Community's Directives on the transit of electricity and gas will facilitate movement of these energy sources within the Community. In the electricity sector, competition may increase as the Directive makes it easier to import or export electricity throughout the Community. In the gas sector, it will open up opportunities to supply to other utilities.

### Liberalisation of gas and electricity markets

These two proposed Directives – currently under discussion – would grant large energy users and distribution companies direct access to grids. Extension of cost transparency through unbundling of accounts could give your competitors and existing large customers enhanced knowledge of your pricing policies. These developments might have an effect on how you need to market your company.

### Price transparency

The Directive ensuring electricity and gas supply companies provide data, for publication, on prices charged to different classes of industrial consumer will affect the knowledge your customers have of your own tariff policies and those of your competitors. This could affect your market position.

### Energy efficiency

A European Community Decision on the SAVE programme provides a framework designed to improve the efficiency of energy use. The Commission has proposed measures which include stricter technical standards, energy labelling requirements, and measures to remove institutional barriers to energy efficiency. This affects the knowledge that your customers have of the efficiency of your products, and this could impact on your market share. You may want to change your marketing strategy in order to take account of this increased awareness.

## Further information

Turn to the Energy topic at p. 175 in Volume 2 for more detailed coverage of these measures.

# 1.11 Environmental policy

## Are you affected?

Your business is affected if:

- you have a product which could be considered to be 'environmentally friendly';
- you or your competitors have a product which, when produced, used or disposed of, could be considered harmful to the environment.

## Why?

A Regulation from the Commission sets out the procedure for the award of ecolabels for environmentally less damaging products. In the UK the scheme is administered by the United Kingdom Ecolabelling Board. This will consider applications for the ecolabel against strict criteria and promote the scheme nationally.

## How?

The main ways in which the sales and marketing function will be affected by environmental policy are:

### Ecolabels

The introduction of an ecolabel means that you may gain significant competitive advantage if your product(s) were to be awarded an ecolabel. This is because consumers are becoming increasingly aware of, and sophisticated in their response to, 'green' issues: environmental claims will no longer be as credible in the market place unless they are supported by the ecolabel. You should therefore find out more about the criteria which would be used to judge your product and the application procedure.

## Further information

Turn to the Environmental policy topic at p. 185 in Volume 2 for more detailed coverage of this measure.

# 1.12 Consumer protection

## Are you affected?

Your business is affected if:

- you are a retailer and you sell products in bulk;
- you offer consumer credit;
- you promote your own products and/or services;
- you promote your products and/or services through distance selling (for example, mail order).

## Why?

- Recent legislation requires you to specify unit prices on products which are sold in bulk, in order to enable consumers to make direct cost and value comparisons.
- Recent Community legislation establishes a common method for calculating the APR (annual percentage rate of charge) for consumer credit, although it also enables pre-March 1990 formulae to continue to be used. In member states which have implemented the Directive, you will be required to use the common EC formula for calculating the APR of consumer credit offered. If you intend to provide consumer credit in another EC member state, you should seek advice on what rules apply there in respect of the APR calculation.
- The proposed tightening of data protection laws across the Community could significantly affect the way in which products and services can be marketed within member states. If the proposal for a data protection Directive is adopted in its current form, direct mail and list broking could become virtually impossible, making it particularly difficult for companies who undertake direct marketing operations such as mail order.

    In addition, under proposed data protection laws, firms would no longer be able to buy customer lists or create their own databases for mailing purposes without the permission of all individuals to be held on the system. Mail order operations would be seriously affected.
- If Community Directives on data protection and distance selling are adopted, Community firms who promote their products or services through:
    - ★ mail order;
    - ★ telephone and fax selling; and
    - ★ other forms of promotion where the contract to sell is made without face-to-face contact;

    will find these 'distance selling' activities regulated in more detail in the future.

## How?

The main ways in which the sales and marketing function will be affected by EC consumer protection measures are:

### Easier comparison of prices

The two price indication Directives require that the selling price, and, in some cases, the unit price of most food and non-food products be displayed. Unit prices have to be shown for goods which are either measured from bulk in the presence of the customer or pre-packed in variable (random) quantities and, in some cases, when pre-packed in fixed quantities.

### Common EC formula for calculating the APR for consumer credit

An amendment to the consumer credit Directive, concerning a common method for calculating the APR (annual percentage rate of charge) for consumer credit came into effect at the end of 1992. However, some member states, including the UK, are taking advantage of transitional provisions in the Directive allowing them to postpone implementation until 31 December 1995. The existing Consumer Credit (Total Charge for Credit) Regulations 1980 will therefore continue to apply in the UK until further notice.

### Restrictions on distance selling

The proposal on distance selling, for example, mail order, aims to regulate certain types of sales agreements where the contract is agreed without face-to-face contact between buyer and supplier at any stage.

The sorts of promotional activity to be affected are likely to be direct mail, sale or return, televised promotional offers, mail order, electronic mail and telephone selling.

If the proposal is implemented, businesses who practise distance selling may have to:

- incur the costs of complying with the requirements of the Directive;
- consider other forms of marketing communications.

### Data protection proposals

The current proposals on data protection would make selective direct marketing very difficult since it would:

- only allow database listings to be sold on with the agreement of all the people named on the list; and
- prevent 'profiling', whereby information about individuals is drawn together from a number of different sources.

In addition, the proposal would extend legislation to cover areas currently exempt from the UK's Data Protection Act. These are:

- structured collections of manual data;
- data held for payroll, pensions and accounts purposes.

If this proposal were adopted in its present form, businesses:

- might have to use more expensive, less cost-effective methods of marketing communication;
- would have to be more aware of the legislative requirements to ensure their promotional activities do not lead to prosecution;
- would have to look to ensure that direct mail becomes more 'user friendly', losing its 'junk mail' reputation, to support their case for a balance between rights to privacy and effective targeted marketing.

The proposal on data protection is highly contentious and is likely to be amended before any Directive is adopted by the Council. The UK government does not support the proposal as it stands, as it goes beyond the European Convention on Data Protection. The UK is a signatory to the Convention, and existing UK data protection laws are based on it.

## Further information

Turn to the Consumer protection topic at p. 203 in Volume 2 for more detailed coverage of these measures and proposals.

# 1.13 Intellectual property

## Are you affected?

Your business is affected if:

- you sell products or services in other member states for which you own patents or trade marks;
- you manufacture, sell or license computer programs.

## Why?

- In order to promote the free movement of goods and services, the Community is seeking to ensure the protection of patents and trade marks on a Community-wide basis.

    The Community Patent Convention will make it possible to obtain a single patent valid in all member states. A Directive harmonising those provisions of national laws relating to trade marks which have the most direct effect on the free movement of goods and services has been adopted. The Community has proposed the creation of a Community trade mark applicable in all member states. These measures should facilitate trade in the Community.

- A Directive has also been adopted to harmonise software copyright laws in the member states to ensure a common standard of protection for computer programs. The software Directive will ensure that computer programs are protected under copyright as literary works throughout the Community and that the unauthorised copying of a program is infringement of copyright in the program. Ideas and principles underlying a program, including those underlying its interface, are not protected.

## How?

The main ways in which the sales and marketing function in your organisation may be affected by EC intellectual property measures are:

### Community patent

Under the Community Patent Convention the introduction of a patent valid in all member states will eliminate the multiple procedures required to maintain a patent in each of the member states.

Community patents will simplify renewal arrangements for patent protection in the Community. Moreover, the Convention will establish a system of law, common to all contracting states, for the determination of matters relating to infringement and validity of Community patents.

### National trade mark laws

The harmonisation of trade mark law in the Community will ensure that the conditions for obtaining and maintaining a registered trade mark are the same in all member states. This may make markets which previously had lower trade mark protection more viable and attractive. However, whilst national trade mark laws continue to exist, there will remain potential sources of conflict between identical or similar trade marks governed by such legislation and held by different owners. You may therefore still be refused access to a market because one of your competitors owns a similar trade mark to your own.

### Community trade mark

The creation of a Community trade mark issued by a single Community office (the Community Trade Mark Office) will give you, as a trade mark owner, the exclusive right to use your mark throughout the Community. This should make it easier to extend your promotional activities in all member states. However, registration of a Community trade mark could be refused on the grounds that a prior conflicting right has been granted to a competitor in one member state, either by virtue of legislation or use. If this is the case, the only protection available to you will be separate registration in the member states concerned.

You should be aware that the implementation of such a trade mark has been long delayed by difficulties over the linguistic, financial and locational arrangements for the Community Trade Mark Office.

The Community trade mark will exist in parallel with national systems, so if you seek national coverage only for your products or services, you will still be able to take the less expensive option of applying solely for a national trade mark.

### The software Directive

The Software Directive allows decompilation (or reverse engineering) of a program without authorisation of the copyright owner to reproduce and translate its code in order to achieve interoperability of programs, thus allowing customers to make your program compatible with your competitors' products.

This exception to the rights of the copyright owner, however, is strictly limited to achieving interoperability, and must not be used for the development of a program substantially similar in its expression to that of the decompiled program. It is also only allowed where the information to achieve interoperability is not previously readily available.

Provision is also made in the Directive for the correction of program errors and the making of back-up copies. The Copyright (Computer Programs) Regulations 1992 implement the Directive and you should study this to determine the rights of your customers.

You may wish to seek expert advice on the decompilation right to ensure that your customers comply with the Directive.

## Further information

Turn to the Intellectual property topic at p. 225 in Volume 2 for more detailed coverage of these measures and proposals.

# 1.14 Information technologies and telecommunications

## Are you affected?

Your business is affected if:

- you use personal information held on computer or other filing system in the course of marketing your product or service;
- you are responsible for your company's publicity material;
- you produce advertisements for television broadcast;
- you gather and exchange information electronically, or it could be useful for you to do so.

## Why?

- The Commission's proposals regarding personal data protection are intended to make sure that the handling of personal data, whether computerised or manual, does not infringe privacy rights. If the proposals are adopted in their present form, the use of customer databases will be more restricted than at present.
- You should be aware that the EC is introducing a series of common telephone numbers across Europe, such as a standard emergency services number, and a common international access code. Your publicity material may need to be changed to incorporate this.
- The Directive on Community-wide transmission of broadcasts affects advertising content as well as programme content. The provisions of the Directive are encompassed in the current Independent Television Commission (ITC) codes.
- The Commission is funding two programmes aimed at promoting the development of new kinds of information services. One is the Trade Electronic Data Interchange Systems (TEDIS) programme which promotes electronic data interchange (EDI – the exchange of data between computer systems) throughout the EC and EFTA countries. The second is the Information Market Policy Actions (IMPACT) programme. It aims to promote the single market for electronic information services, and includes actions to overcome legal and administrative barriers, increase user-friendliness, improve information literacy, and support information initiatives.

    Both programmes operate through calls for proposals for collaborative projects. EDI could be an important medium for you to use in the gathering of information, if you do not use it already.

# INFORMATION TECHNOLOGY AND TELECOMMUNICATIONS · 31
## How?

The main ways in which the sales and marketing function will be affected by EC information technologies and telecommunications policy are:

### Customers

Current proposals on data protection would restrict your use of market information, including use of direct mailing techniques, approaching potential customers on the basis of information from other sources, transfer of data to non-Community countries, and possibly the extent and type of access to information from other parts of the organisation. The UK's Data Protection Act 1984 already regulates the use of computerised personal data, but, in accordance with principles of proper handling and transparency, not privacy. The UK government's position on these proposals is that those parts of it which go beyond the Convention on Data Protectoin, and, therefore, the Data Protection Act, are unnecessary. Agreement on the Commission's proposals may take considerable time.

### Publicity

Changes in telephone numbers, as with the conversion of the London code from 01 to 071 or 081, may require changes or alterations to be made both to external publicity material, and to internal materials containing company details.

The Council has adopted Decisions to introduce '00' as the harmonised international access code and '112' as the single European emergency call number. '00' will be introduced in the UK as part of the national numbering plan change at Easter 1995. The single emergency number will be introduced in parallel with the existing '999' number by 31 December 1992.

### Advertising

There are restrictions concerning the amount of advertising which a broadcaster may carry and the content of those advertisements. These provisions are reflected in the current ITC codes.

### EDI and other information services

Information exchange services, including EDI, allow businesses to provide new services such as tele-shopping direct to consumers through telephone links. These may be a useful new way for you to pursue your sales or marketing strategies. However, information exchange may also be subject to increasingly stringent data protection rules. This is covered in Chapter 15 (Intellectual Property) in Volume 2. However, the freer exchange of information generally, and easier access to customers, suppliers, and so on, depends upon the harmonisation of telecommunications and other electronics standards, which is part of an ongoing process.

# 32 • THE SALES AND MARKETING FUNCTION

## Further information

Turn to the Information technologies and telecommunications topic at p. 239 in Volume 2 for more detailed coverage of these measures and proposals.

# 1.15 Company law

## Are you affected?

Your business is affected if:

- you have links with firms in other member states which you wish to develop.

## Why?

The Community has created a framework for co-operation between businesses from different member states called the European Economic Interest Grouping (EEIG). The EEIG is designed to help companies, firms or individuals establish and maintain links with businesses in other member states, without merging or forming a joint subsidiary.

## How?

The main way in which the sales and marketing function will be affected by EC company law is:

### Customers

The EEIG is a new form of business organisation aimed at providing a common framework for cross-border co-operation in certain activities.

An EEIG could be used for joint selling or marketing activities. It may facilitate access to markets and consumers in other member states.

## Further information

Turn to the Company law topic at p. 265 in Volume 2 for more detailed coverage of this measure.

# 1.16 Financial services

## Are you affected?
Your business is affected if:
- you sell to providers of financial and/or investment services;
- you operate in other member states.

## Why?
- There is a considerable amount of technical legislation affecting financial and investment services providers within the Community, but its overall objective is to facilitate the general opening up of Community markets by enabling firms to offer their services freely throughout the Community.
- The Directive harmonising the requirements for annual and consolidated accounts of banks and other financial institutions will make it easier for companies to compare the accounts of current and potential customers from different member states. The Directive excludes insurance companies, which are covered by a separate Directive.
- Exchange controls have been abolished in most Community countries under the capital liberalisation Directive, which may make these markets more attractive for business purposes. Greece has until June 1994 to abolish remaining restrictions.

## How?
The main ways in which the sales and marketing function will be affected by EC financial services measures are:

### The opening up of the financial services sector
As a result of current and proposed Community legislation, it is increasingly likely that providers of financial and investment services will:
- look to develop their client base at Community level, in addition to domestic level;
- develop Community-wide branch networks, should this option offer the most effective form of distribution; and
- require a wider range of suppliers in order to meet their requirements for products and services on a broader geographical basis.

Although different financial sectors are likely to respond in different ways to the opening up of Community markets, it will be important for you to understand the legislation affecting your financial sector customers, and to ensure you can meet their future requirements should they decide to expand their European operations.

### The free movement of capital

The capital liberalisation Directive enables the free movement of capital across the Community, and will result in the removal of remaining exchange controls.

The Directive also includes a declaration of intent that member states should liberalise capital flows with any non-EC country.

### Harmonisation of accounting requirements

The bank accounts Directive harmonises the requirements for banks and other financial institutions in the preparation of their annual and consolidated accounts.

The ability to make more direct financial comparisons between banks in other member states as a result of this harmonisation should assist you, or banks and credit-rating agencies, to assess the finanical standing of current and potential customers more effectively.

The implementation of the bank branches Directive, alongside the eleventh company law Directive means that, if you are dealing with a branch of a bank in the UK which is incorporated in another member state, you will be able to obtain copies of the accounts of that bank from Companies House. (For more details see Chapter 17 (Company Law) in Volume 2).

## Further information

Turn to the Financial services topic at p. 299 in Volume 2 for more detailed coverage of these measures and proposals.

# 1.17 Insurance

## Are you affected?

Your business is affected if:

- you sell to firms selling insurance.

## Why?

- Community legislation affecting the insurance industry is similar to that affecting the other branches of the financial services sector, to the extent that its overall objective is to open up the Community markets by enabling all member state insurers to offer their products freely throughout the EC. This should provide you with a wider choice of customers in the insurance sector, as more firms enter the UK market. In addition, current customers may wish to expand into other member states, providing you with increased sales opportunities.

   A Directive prescribes the information which should be included in the annual accounts of all Community insurers. This complements the bank accounts Directive, enabling companies (from 1995 onwards) to compare the accounts of current and potential customers from different member states.

## How?

The main ways in which the sales and marketing function in your organisation may be affected by EC insurance measures are:

### Customers

Although the UK insurance market is already among the most liberal in the Community, the completion of the single market is likely to lead to an increase in competition, as:

- UK insurers look to expand at Community level, whilst consolidating their position on a domestic level;
- EC insurance companies enter the UK market, on the basis of their home state authorisation.

In response to these changes, it is important for you to understand how legislation may affect your current and future customers. Customers deciding to expand their European operations may need a wider range of suppliers in order to meet their requirements on a broader geographical basis. Insurers unable to compete in the new environment may be squeezed out of the market.

### Easier comparison of accounts

The accounts Directive establishes a framework for common standards of accounting for all insurance undertakings with a head office in a member state (whether incorporated or not). These provisions will apply to the accounts of insurance undertakings for financial years beginning during 1995 and subsequent years. Member states may extend the provisions of the accounts Directive to branches of insurance companies which have their head offices outside the EC.

The ability to make more direct financial comparisons between firms throughout the single market as a result of these common standards should assist you, or banks and credit-rating agencies, in assessing more effectively the financial standing of current and potential customers, and reduce the risk of bad debts.

## Further information

Turn to the Insurance topic at p. 319 in Volume 2 for more detailed coverage of these measures.

# 1.18 State aids

## Are you affected?

Your business is affected if:

- you face unfair competition as a result of subsidies, or other distorting aid, to companies in other countries.

## Why?

The Commission has considerable powers to monitor and limit all forms of aid and support from member states that potentially distort competition in the Community. Although some regional and other kinds of aid are authorised (generally within clear limits and conditions), there may be grounds for making a complaint to the Commission if you face unfairly subsidised or assisted competitors.

## How?

The main way in which the sales and marketing function may be affected by EC state aids policy is in its impact on your competitive position:

### Competitors

Market research and gathering information about competitors may enable you to find out whether any of your competitors is receiving unfair state aid. You should consider the impact on your competitive position and ensure that such abuse is reported to the Commission.

You may wish to discuss this first with your trade association or the DTI. You will need to bear in mind, however, that not all state aid is illegal. The majority of aid offered by other member states will have been approved by the Commission. You will also need to remember that the Commission is unable to act on the basis of rumour or hearsay. Substantive evidence of the unfair effect on competition will be required.

## Further information

Turn to the State aids topic at p. 333 in Volume 2 for more detailed coverage of this measure.

# 1.19 Structural funds

## Are you affected?

Your business is affected if:

- you or your clients sell products or services to areas which have traditionally produced coal or steel, in one of the least prosperous regions of the Community, or in a rural area;
- you or your customers are small or medium-sized enterprises.

## Why?

- The European Coal and Steel Community (ECSC) offers financial assistance to companies in the form of grants, loans and guarantees to improve economic and social conditions in coal and steel producing regions. The European Regional Development Fund provides support, via the DTI, for industrial investment in small firms in designated areas, and via the Department of Environment and the Scottish and Welsh Offices for infrastructure projects, local initiatives, studies, technical assistance, pilot schemes, and environmental protection measures. Funding is also available, via the Ministry for Agriculture, Fisheries and Food (MAFF), for agricultural and fishery developments.
- The European Investment Bank (EIB) offers cheap loans for small and medium-sized enterprises and other larger firms for projects which further the development of the Community.

## How?

The main way in which the sales and marketing function may be affected by structural funds is:

### Financial assistance

Structural funds, the EIB and the ECSC provide financial assistance for certain types of project or specified geographic areas. This assistance could open up new marketing and sales opportunities.

## Further information

Turn to the Structural funds topic at p. 343 in Volume 2 for more detailed coverage of this measure.

# 1.20 Competition policy

## Are you affected?

Your business is affected if:

- you are involved, or intend to become involved, in a franchise agreement;
- you are involved, or intend to become involved, in an exclusive distribution agreement.

## Why?

Article 85 of the Treaty of Rome prohibits agreements between firms, decisions by associations of firms and concerted practices which prevent, restrict or distort competition in the Community if trade between member states may be affected. Agreements meeting certain conditions may be exempted from the prohibition in Art. 85, and most agreements between small firms are not affected by Community competition rules. The Community has also adopted block exemption Regulations which exempt, amongst other things, some exclusive distribution agreements and some franchise agreements from Art. 85.

## How?

The main ways in which the sales and marketing function will be affected by EC competition policy are:

### Franchising

The franchise block exemption Regulation, which exempts some franchise agreements from the prohibition in Art. 85, sets out the restrictions which may and those which may not be imposed on the franchisee or franchisor.

If you already have a franchise agreement, it is important to ensure that your agreement complies with the rules of the Regulation. You should be aware that if your agreement does not comply with the rules of the Regulation, it will, if it infringes Art. 85, be automatically void. The Commission can withdraw an exemption from an agreement in certain circumstances, for example, where there is a lack of adequate competition. You may need to obtain specialist legal advice.

If you are a small organisation, many of the franchise agreements you conclude with similar sized companies will not be considered as infringing Art. 85.

### Exclusive distribution agreements

The block exemption Regulation which exempts some exclusive distribution agreements from the prohibition in Art. 85 sets out the restrictions which may and those which may not be imposed on the distributor.

The exclusive distribution block exemption covers agreements where one party is given a territory in which only he/she is allowed to sell the goods supplied by the other party. However, the supplier is not allowed to guarantee absolute territorial protection to the distributor, for example by preventing the importation by another distributor of goods obtained from a third party outside the territory ('parallel importing').

Active selling by the distributor outside his allocated territory may also be banned, but passive selling by the distributor responding to unsolicited requests by customers in other territories may not be prevented by the supplier.

You should be aware that if your agreement does not comply with the rules of the Regulation, it will, if it infringes Art. 85, be automatically void. In some circumstances, the Commission may withdraw exemption from an agreement under the Regulation. You may need to obtain specialist legal advice.

## Further information

Turn to the Competition policy topic at p. 351 in Volume 2 for more detailed coverage of these measures and proposals.

# 1.21 Food law

## Are you affected?

Your business is affected if:

- you retail fresh or processed food in the UK or elsewhere in the Community;
- you wholesale fresh or processed food in the UK or elsewhere in the Community;
- you retail or wholesale food additives in the UK or elsewhere in the Community.

## Why?

Community framework Directives are now in place covering materials in contact with food, labelling, presentation and advertising, foods for particular nutritional uses, additives and flavourings, the official control of foodstuffs, hygiene of foodstuffs and contaminants in food.

## How?

The main ways in which the sales and marketing function will be affected by EC food law are:

### Materials in contact with food

This legislation, in force in the UK since 1987, is aimed at minimising any health risks to consumers from contamination of food by substances transferring from the materials in contact with it. Both pre-packed and loose foods should only come into contact with materials manufactured in accordance with this legislation.

### Labelling, presentation and advertising

This Directive, fully in force in the UK since 1984, sets out standard rules relating to the labelling, presentation and advertising of foodstuffs for sale to the ultimate consumer and includes quantity marking provisions. The rules have since been extended to require alcoholic strength marking, to harmonise date marking, and to require labelling to indicate if a food has undergone irradiation. Rules for nutrition labelling will take effect fully on 1 October 1993, but may be observed now. Detailed controls on nutrition and other claims that manufacturers may make about their products have yet to be negotiated, meanwhile national rules continue to apply.

### Foods for particular nutritional uses

This Directive, adopted in May 1989, covers infant and follow-on formulae, baby foods, low-energy foods, dietary foods for special medical purposes, low-sodium foods, gluten-free foods, foods for sports people, and diabetic foods. Regulations made under the Food Safety Act 1990 will come into force in Great Britain in 1993. Similar arrangements will apply in Northern Ireland.

The Directive includes consumer-protection clauses relating to the claims manufacturers can make about the properties of their products.

### Food additives and flavourings

These Directives, in force in the UK since September 1992, lay down the general safety and labelling requirements for food additives and flavourings sold at wholesale and retail level. All additives and flavourings should comply with the requirements of this legislation.

### The official control of foodstuffs

This Directive, in force in the UK since 1991, allows member states to carry out inspections at all stages of the manufacturing and distribution chain to ensure that Community food law is complied with.

The same rules apply to food for export to other member states and to third countries.

### Contaminants in food

A common position has been reached on this proposed Regulation which lays down a procedure for setting limits on contaminants in foods. Subsequent measures on specific contaminants will be proposed by the Commission. Contaminants which are the subject of more specific Community rules, such as pesticides and veterinary medicines, are not covered by this Regulation.

### Hygiene of foodstuffs

A common position has been reached on this proposed Directive which would establish general hygiene principles to be followed by all food businesses. It would cover the production and all other processes through to sale of foodstuffs to the final consumer. The provisions of the Directive are broadly similar to existing requirements of UK law.

# Further information

Turn to the Food law topic at p. 373 in Volume 2 for more detailed coverage of these measures and proposals.

# 1.22 Pharmaceuticals

## Are you affected?

Your business is affected if:

- you sell medicinal products for human or veterinary use;
- you manufacture and package medicinal products for human or veterinary use;
- you advertise medicinal products for human use.

## Why?

1. *Products for human or veterinary use*
- The Council of Ministers has reached agreement on a package of proposals, known as 'Future Systems', which, probably from 1995, will begin to harmonise licensing decisions across the Community. There will be a centralised procedure for certain types of new medicines, such as those derived from biotechnology, whereby licensing decisions will be made by Community bodies and will be binding in all member states. For all other medicines (except homoeopathics), a decentralised procedure will operate, based on mutual recognition of national licensing decisions, with binding arbitration by Community bodies where member states disagree over a decision. National licensing procedures will continue to apply in respect of products which are to be marketed only in the member state where they are authorised. The new procedures will be supported by a European Medicines Evaluation Agency (EMEA).
- The Community has also agreed a set of Community-wide criteria to determine whether or not a medicinal product should be restricted to supply on prescription. These measures should go some way towards eliminating differences between member states in classifying medicines for retail supply.
- The Community has adopted a number of provisions regarding the labelling of medicinal products and the information published on package leaflets. These provisions specify the particulars to appear on the outer packaging of the product and on the 'immediate packaging', together with details of how this information should be presented.

2. *Products for human use only*
- Disparities in national pricing systems for medicines greatly affect intra-Community trade in pharmaceuticals. In order to remove barriers to trade, and thus stimulate free competition, the Community has agreed standards for transparency in national authorities' criteria in setting prices for medicinal products for human use.

- In order to improve information available to consumers regarding pharmaceuticals, the Community has outlined the conditions that medicine advertisements of all types have to meet, and the kinds of information which are prohibited from being advertised. This may affect your advertising strategy.

## How?

The main ways in which the sales and marketing function will be affected by pharmaceuticals measures are:

1. *For products for human or veterinary use*

### Product licences

The proposed Community licensing procedures ('Future Systems') should, in due course, lessen the delays and administrative burden involved in seeking licences in more than one member state, and reduce differences in the licences granted by individual member states.

Future Systems should give you easier access to EC markets. It is also likely to sharpen competition in your home market.

### Classification

The Directive on classification for the supply of medicinal products for human use – and parallel provisions in Directives on veterinary medicinal products – aim to harmonise the conditions for the retail supply of medicinal products. Member states are required to classify medicines for human use into prescription and non-prescription categories and to provide a list of those restricted to supply on prescription in their country.

### Labelling

If you market medicinal products in the EC, from 1 January 1994 you will have to comply with the requirements of the Directives on the labelling of such products. In particular, a package leaflet addressed primarily to the patient, or in the case of veterinary medicines to the veterinary surgeon or user, will have to be included, unless all the required information is directly conveyed on the labelling. Such leaflets will also have to comply with the requirements of the Directives.

2. *For products for human use only*

### Pricing of products

Transparency of pricing measures in the Community will make it more difficult for one member state's national authorities to put products from another member state at a disadvantage by delaying decisions on price applications, and awarding them uncompetitive prices. This should make it easier to detect discrimination and thus allow you to defend your interests.

Transparency of pricing measures are generally expected to result in a convergence of prices in the Community. In particular, it should discourage parallel importing, where products purchased in a lower-priced member state are sold in a higher-priced one.

## Advertising

Advertising of medicinal products, as defined in the Directive, encompasses information of any kind directed to the public or to health-care professionals, and sales promotions. In these areas, the Directive broadly endorses many of the arrangements which already apply in the UK.

You should be aware, however, that the Directive also covers the giving by pharmaceutical companies, or acceptance by professionals, of gifts, financial inducements and offers of hospitality, and regulates the activities of pharmaceutical company sales representatives.

# Further information

Turn to the Pharmaceuticals topic at p. 381 in Volume 2 for more detailed coverage of these measures and proposals.

# 2 · The **PURCHASING** function

| | | |
|---|---|---|
| 2.1 | **Transport** | 49 |
| 2.2 | **Excise duties** | 53 |
| 2.3 | **Frontier controls** | 55 |
| 2.4 | **Trade policy and customs duties** | 56 |
| 2.5 | **Freedom of movement for workers** | 58 |
| 2.6 | **Public procurement** | 59 |
| 2.7 | **Energy** | 62 |
| 2.8 | **Environmental policy** | 64 |
| 2.9 | **Information technologies and telecommunications** | 65 |
| 2.10 | **Financial services** | 67 |
| 2.11 | **Insurance** | 69 |
| 2.12 | **Food law** | 71 |
| 2.13 | **Pharmaceuticals** | 73 |

# 2.1 Transport

## Are you affected?

Your business is affected if:
- you purchase freight transport services;
- you purchase road haulage services;
- you purchase water freight services;
- you purchase rail freight services;
- you purchase air freight services.

## Why?

- Whether you currently import from other member states or not, there are likely to be reductions in transport times and costs as a result of the liberalisation of Community freight transport services. Firms who take advantage of these changes in the road, rail, air and water transport industries and who choose the most effective mode(s) of transport should be able to access more competitive, possibly non-UK suppliers.
- Although the costs of internal UK road haulage are unlikely to change significantly in real terms, the abolition of quotas and permits for international services within the Community and the freedom for road hauliers to access all Community countries will bring about reductions in the cost of cross-border road haulage services.

  The Community is also aiming to promote the use of 'combined' (multi-modal) transport. This involves unitised freight starting and finishing its journey on the road, but travelling for the most part by rail or by water. It is hoped that this will be a faster, more cost-effective means of transport which will also be less damaging to the environment.
- The liberalisation of the inland waterways and maritime freight transport industry should enable you to purchase more effective, community-wide transport services, as:
  * Community water freight firms are able to offer services in any member state;
  * firms are, as a result, subjected to increased competition from new, non-domestic water freight transporters.
- Users of rail freight are likely to see improvements in the cost and speed of this form of transport as:
  * the Channel Tunnel prepares to open in 1993;
  * access to the EC rail network is opened up to undertakings operating international combined transport services.
- Air freight services have been fully liberalised, which is likely to benefit you as:
  * new operators enter the market and new routes are opened up;

★ cargo rates become more competitive.

Some restructuring within the industry is possible, as less competitive firms are forced to respond to new market conditions.

# How?

The main ways in which the Purchasing function will be affected by transport measures are:

## A wider choice of suppliers

The Community has adopted a number of measures and is examining others enabling companies to offer transport services freely throughout the Community. This liberalisation is likely to lead to:

- increased competition in all transport sectors;
- a downward pressure on margins;
- some industry restructuring, with a potential increase in concentration within the UK industry.

For your business, these improvements are likely to mean that:

- through the use of improved transport, you will be able to access more cost-effective, possibly non-UK suppliers;
- product profitability could be improved should you renegotiate the transport cost component of your suppliers' prices;
- your range and mix of suppliers could be altered, if appropriate, to take advantage of suppliers who might previously have been geographically inaccessible.

## A more price competitive road haulage sector

UK road hauliers have not been completely free to pick up and deliver loads between other member states or between points in another member state. While there has been free access to some members of the Community – namely Denmark, the Benelux countries, the Republic of Ireland, Portugal and Greece – other member states have limited the transport of goods by road through the use of quotas or permits.

The key element to the liberalisation of the Community's road haulage sector, therefore, has been the abolition of permits and quotas for all international journeys within the Community. This should mean cheaper transport for a large number of Community firms. However, access by road hauliers in one member state to the domestic markets of other member states remains subject to strict quotas.

## Developments in combined transport

Combined transport involves the use of rail or water for the trunk haul of unitised goods with initial pick-up and final delivery carried out by road. It has been a feature of longer distance transport operations in mainland Europe for some years. All British Rail's proposed Channel Tunnel freight terminals are to have intermodal facilities.

The objective of combined transport is to provide a cost-effective alternative to road haulage, while helping to safeguard the environment and assist in increasing rail's share of the freight transport market.

In order to encourage the growth of combined transport, the Commission has proposed an indicative network of international freight routes. This would involve substantial investment in the Community's infrastructure: completion of the basic network would be of the order of ECU 2 billion.

An EC Directive adopted in 1991 provides for open access to the EC rail network for undertakings operating international combined transport services.

## Improvements in maritime freight

The progresive liberalisation of shipping by Community nationals between member states and between member states and third countries was agreed in 1986. In addition, a Regulation has been agreed which will enable Community shipowners (that is, those meeting the ownership/control requirements of the Regulation) whose vessels are registered in a member state, to provide services within member states (cabotage) progressively from 1 January 1993. There are derogations for certain cargoes and trades. This Regulation will end the protected positions enjoyed by some operators in their domestic markets.

## Improvements in rail transport

It is likely that the planned opening of the Channel Tunnel during 1993 will be of most benefit to freight transport from the UK to central and southern Europe, enhancing the time and cost advantages of long-haul rail freight.

Progress towards a unified European rail network has been slow because the disparities between the systems developed by individual national railway companies have presented barriers to fast and efficient inter-operation. The Commission is drafting measures to overcome these barriers in the context of proposals for a European high-speed train network by the gradual introduction of technical compatibility of infrastructure, rolling stock and control and command systems as new lines are constructed and existing ones upgraded. As technical compatibility develops, it is likely to extend to the conventional rail network.

## Improvements in air transport

The Community aims to liberalise the air transport sector further, in line with other forms of transport. Significant progress has been made.

The key areas are:

- *air carrier licensing*: as from 1 January 1992, uniform criteria have applied throughout the Community to assess the financial and technical fitness of air carriers proposing to operate within the single market. These criteria replace national licensing regimes and any carrier meeting these criteria will be entitled to an operating licence;
- *market access*: as from 1 January 1993 Community airlines are allowed to operate services between all Community airports, subject only to transitional arrangements affecting services operated wholly within another member state;

- *pricing*: as from 1 January 1993, air carriers may set scheduled fares according to market conditions, subject to certain safeguards against exploitative or predatory practices. Cargo rates and fares for non-scheduled services remain unrestricted.
- *slot allocation*: a Regulation adopted in December 1992 improves the transparency, neutrality and efficiency of the system whereby take-off and landing slots at congested Community airports are allocated between airlines.

## Further information

Turn to the Transport topic at p. 27 in Volume 2 for more detailed coverage of these measures and proposals.

## 2.2 Excise duties

### Are you affected?

Your business is affected if:

- you purchase commercial quantities of excisable goods such as cigarettes, alcoholic drinks and mineral oils.

### Why?

The agreement to set minimum rates and to harmonise the structures of duties on cigarettes, wines, spirits and mineral oils could affect prices in some member states.

### How?

The main ways in which the purchasing function is affected by EC excise duties policy are:

#### Cigarettes

The agreement for a minimum rate of 57 per cent of retail price (including tax) in the most popular price category per 1,000 cigarettes may mean increases in the cost of cigarettes in some member states. This could result in reduced demand or increased costs for companies if they choose to absorb some of the extra cost of the duty. Spain, Italy, Greece and France needed to increase taxes on cigarettes to meet the minimum rate.

#### Beer

Luxembourg, France, Spain and Portugal needed to increase excise duty to meet the agreed minimum of ECU 1.87 for every degree of alcohol per 1,000 litres. This could result in increased prices in these countries.

#### Cider and perry

The agreement classifies cider and perry as 'other fermented beverages' (not beer or wine) which may be liable to a reduced duty rate. This has allowed the UK to retain its existing duty structure.

#### Spirits

A minimum rate of ECU 550 per hectolitre of pure alcohol (hlpa) was agreed for spirits. However member states who previously applied a rate not exceeding ECU 1,000 per hlpa may not reduce it. In addition, member states who previously applied a rate in excess of ECU 1,000 per hlpa may not reduce it below ECU 1,000. This agreement did not require any member state to increase its duty on spirits.

### Still and sparkling wine

A minimum rate of zero was set for wines.

Sales in high-duty member states could be affected by cross-border shopping, as consumers take advantage of the abolition of frontier controls to purchase cheaper goods.

### Intermediate products

A minimum duty rate for intermediate products (fortified beverages such as vermouth) of ECU 45 per hectolitre of product was agreed. This required Portugal to increase its duty on these products.

### Mineral oils

- *Diesel*: the agreed minimum rate of excise on diesel could lead to an alteration of relative pricing within the Community.
- *Heating fuels*: the minimum duty for heating oils was set at ECU 18 per 1,000 litres. However, those member states which applied a zero rate on 1 January 1991 may continue to do so, provided they apply a control levy of ECU 5 per 1,000 litres as from 1 January 1993. This charge may be increased to ECU 10 per 1,000 litres on 1 January 1995 if problems of trade distortion are identified.
- *Leaded and unleaded petrol*: the minimum excise rate for unleaded petrol was set at ECU 50 below that of leaded (respectively ECU 287 and ECU 337 per 1,000 litres). These rates are below the current UK rate, so no change to the UK rate was required as a result of this agreement.

## Further information

Turn to the Excise duties topic at p. 63 in Volume 2 for more detailed coverage of these measures.

# 2.3 Frontier controls

## Are you affected?

Your business is affected if:

- you purchase products in the UK or any other member state.

## Why?

With the abolition of border controls on the transportation of goods between member states at the beginning of 1993, firms should be benefiting from a wider choice of price-competitive products, possibly from non-UK suppliers. The removal of these controls is likely to reduce the transport costs and delays which they caused, so suppliers should now have the opportunity to improve the efficiency of their product distribution and consider supplying more geographically distant customers.

## How?

### Reduced costs and transportation times

The overall objective of the Community's frontier controls legislation is to abolish restrictions on the free movement of goods between member states. To facilitate this, the Community drew up a two-stage system, the first stage being effective from 1 January 1988.

The key element of the first stage was that all member states would recognise a single administrative document (SAD) for customs clearance purposes. This simplified the paperwork involved in transporting goods between member states. Previously, as many as 70 different forms needed to be completed.

Stage two involved the co-ordination of policies and the adoption of common legislation to allow the complete elimination of internal frontiers and controls on the movement of goods, including the SAD. This happened at the end of 1992.

These initiatives, combined with the improvements under way in the Community's transport industries, are likely to lead to transport costs being reduced by up to five per cent and transport times being reduced by up to 30 per cent, depending on routes taken. (See Chapter 3 (Transport) in Volume 2.)

## Further information

Turn to the Frontier controls topic at p. 69 in Volume 2 for more detailed coverage of this measure.

# 2.4 Trade policy and customs duties

## Are you affected?
Your business is affected if:
- you purchase goods from members of the European Free Trade Association (EFTA)?

## Why?
The Community's European Economic Area (EEA) agreement with the EFTA countries should make trade between the Community and EFTA easier.

The EC is a customs union, and decisions on changes in the Community's commercial policy and the Common External Tariff (CET) are therefore taken at Community level. Developments in the Community's international trading agreements mean that detailed changes to preferential tariffs and trade arrangements may be made (possibly resulting in increased prices on some imported goods).

Any imposition of anti-dumping or countervailing duties on particular products imported from outside the Community would increase their cost.

## How?
The main ways in which the purchasing function will be affected by EC trade and customs duties policy are:

### The EEA agreement
The formation of the EEA may make markets within the EFTA countries more attractive to you. The EEA will not create a customs union as exists between the member states of the Community, so minimal border formalities will continue. However, many of the non-tariff barriers to trade will be removed, making it easier to trade in EFTA markets.

### Rules of origin
Manufactured goods are often processed in more than one country, making it unclear which country they originate from. Rules of origin are used to establish this, as it is necessary to know the origin of the goods so that the correct customs treatment can be applied. If you import products from EFTA countries, or manufacture goods using imported components, you may find that these goods are still not classified as being of EEA origin if a substantial amount of the processing of the material has taken place outside the Community and EFTA or if the raw material has been obtained outside the EEA and has not been sufficiently worked or processed within the EEA.

### Anti-dumping and countervailing duties

Anti-dumping duties are levied on goods imported from outside the Community at below the domestic market price of the goods if they are causing material injury to Community producers. If you purchase goods which subsequently have anti-dumping duties levied against them, the cost of those goods may increase.

Countervailing duties are levied on goods which are subsidised by the exporting country, and similarly you may experience a rise in price.

### Trade agreements due for renegotiation

The General Agreement on Tariffs and Trade, the Multi-Fibre Arrangement, the Lomé Convention and the Community's scheme for the Generalised System of Preferences may all be subject to change in the near future. Draft texts of the Uruguay Round of GATT talks are freely available.

If you currently import goods covered by these agreements from outside the Community, or if you plan to do so in future, your purchasing decisions should be made in the light of these possible changes.

# Further information

Turn to the Trade policy and customs duties topic at p. 79 in Volume 2 for more detailed coverage of these measures.

# 2.5 Freedom of movement for workers

## Are you affected?

Your business is affected if:

- you purchase professional services in more than one member state.

## Why?

In order to complete the single market and, in particular, to eliminate remaining obstacles to freedom of movement for workers, the Community is seeking to ensure the recognition of professional qualifications, that is the right for fully qualified professionals from one member state to be authorised by the corresponding professional body in another member state in order to join their profession and practise in another member state. This should encourage greater competition in the services market.

## How?

The first general Directive on higher education diplomas sets out a system for 'mutual recognition' of professional qualifications which require at least three years degree-level study. It applies to professions which are regulated directly or indirectly by the state including professions regulated by chartered bodies.

This should assist professionals from other member states to be authorised by corresponding professional bodies in the UK in order to practise here. As a user of professional services, the resulting increase in competition in the UK market is likely to benefit you, particularly if the cost of such services fall.

## Further information

Turn to the Freedom of movement for workers topic at p. 89 in Volume 2 for more detailed coverage of this measure.

# 2.6 Public procurement

## Are you affected?

Your business is affected if:

- you purchase supplies, building works or services in central, local or regional government?

The following also apply to private sector organisations:

- you are part of an organisation providing or operating a network which provides or distributes water, electricity, gas, telecommunications or transport to the public;
- you are part of an organisation supplying water, gas or electricity to networks;
- you are part of an organisation with a licence covering exploration or extraction of oil, gas or solid fuel;
- you are part of an organisation operating a port or airport, that is, providing terminal facilities to transport carriers by air, sea or inland waterways;
- you have a contract for building works which are to be more than 50 per cent funded by a public body;
- you are in receipt of Community funding.

## Why?

The EC's public procurement policy aims to open up public sector markets and encourage purchasers to gain cost savings by extending their purchasing base across borders. The rules also apply to certain private-sector organisations, as covered above. The public procurement rules are likely to cause downward pressure on prices as there may be considerable price discrepancies for certain goods between member states and increased competition will improve the competitiveness of suppliers and contractors both within the EC and in world markets.

If your organisation puts up tenders for supplies and works above certain thresholds, you are required by law to observe the rules. Similar rules for services are to be introduced shortly. They are to be backed up by the availability of legal redress for suppliers and contractors.

## How?

If your business is defined as any of the following you have to comply with the public procurement rules:

- central, regional and/or local government;
- other public bodies such as health services and police forces;

**THE PURCHASING FUNCTION · 59**

- any public organisation coming within the GATT agreement on government procurement (GPA);
- a private sector organisation awarding a 'building works' contract receiving funding of more than 50 per cent from one of the above;
- utilities, both publicly and privately owned.

The public procurement laws create a more competitive buying environment by encouraging suppliers from other member states to bid, but they also require you to abide by well-defined procedures.

## Products

These products/services are covered by the public procurement rules:

- building and civil engineering works;
- supplies of goods on purchase or hire;
- a wide range of services such as consultancy and computer services, accounting, cleaning, property maintenance and refuse disposal, from 1 July 1993.

Contracts below the following thresholds will not be covered:

- *Supplies and services*:

  regional and local government: approx. £140,000;

  central government and other bodies covered by GPA: approx. £88,800;
- *Building works including work divided into lots*: approx. £3.5m;
- *Utilities*:

  supplies to the telecommunications sector: approx. £420,000;

  supplies to other sectors: approx. £280,000;

  building works: approx. £3.5m.

The following hierarchy of standards must be used for the public sector:

- national standards implementing European standards; or
- national standards implementing international standards; or
- national standards; or
- any other standards.

The utilities must use:

- national standards implementing European standards;
- other recognised standards.

## Buying procedures

You will have to abide by the following when purchasing:

- *advertising rules*: In the public sector, almost all tenders above the financial threshold must be advertised in the *Official Journal of the European Communities*. This information is also available from Tenders Electronic Daily. In the utilities sector, you can publish the existence of your pre-qualification system;

- *tendering procedures*: purchasers may use open, restricted or (in the utilities sector and, in exceptional cases, in the public sector) negotiated procedures;
- *qualifications*: you may ask suppliers to meet conditions by giving evidence of their business, financial or technical position;
- *award criteria*: the criteria are price alone, or a combination of factors which makes the tender the 'most economically advantageous'. These might include, for example, price, quality and delivery. Purchasers must state in advance what the criteria will be, and abide by them when assessing bids;
- *time limits*: the time between first advertising a tender and the closing date is specified, and can vary between 37 and 52 days, depending on which procedure is used. In certain circumstances necessitating urgency, this can be reduced to 10 days.

## Compliance

The compliance Directives ensure that firms who think they have been harmed by a breach of the rules will have the same level of legal protection in all member states. In the UK, redress will be through the courts.

# Further information

Turn to the Public procurement topic at p. 153 in Volume 2 for more detailed coverage of these measures.

# 2.7 Energy

## Are you affected?

Your business is affected if:

- you purchase significant quantities of energy.

## Why?

The EC is attempting to create the conditions for an internal energy market. This will make it easier for businesses in one member state to buy gas and electricity from another and will increase competition and result in lower energy costs. Prices for gas and electricity will be published twice a year. In the longer term, industrial producers and users may be able to gain access to grids and pipelines.

The Community is also attempting to increase energy efficiency. This will lead to increased energy labelling requirements, and the introduction of more technical standards for energy-using equipment such as boilers.

## How?

The main ways in which the purchasing function will be affected are:

### Transit of electricity and gas

The EC's Directives on the transit of electricity and gas will facilitate cross-country movements of these energy sources. This will mean that your energy supply could originate in another member state which could possibly result in lower energy costs. You should be aware of the Directive when negotiating for supplies.

### Liberalisation of electricity and gas markets

Two proposed Directives – currently under discussion – would take transit a stage further by permitting access to existing grids by major end-users and distribution companies. Coupled with the proposed 'unbundling' of accounts, this could give you more choice in selecting your energy supplier, and help you make more informed purchasing decisions.

### Price transparency

The Directive ensures that electricity and gas supply companies provide data on prices charged to different classes of industrial consumer. These prices are published by the Statistical Office of the European Communities to make it easier for firms to compare their costs over time directly with the costs of other energy sources in the UK and other member states. This could improve the position of large companies when negotiating for supplies.

### Energy efficiency

The Community's Decision on the SAVE programme provides a framework designed to improve the efficiency of energy use. The Commission has proposed measures which include stricter technical standards, energy labelling requirements and measures to remove institutional barriers to energy efficiency. This may increase the prices of these products, but will mean that your energy demand may decrease (assuming everything else stays the same). You may have to take this possible reduction of energy demand into account when you contract for your long-term energy requirements, and also when budgeting for the purchase of energy-using appliances.

## Further information

Turn to the Energy topic at p. 175 in Volume 2 for more detailed coverage of these measures.

## 2.8 Environmental policy

### Are you affected?

Your business is affected if:

- your supplier's products could be considered to be 'environmentally friendly'?

### Why?

A Regulation from the EC sets out the procedure for the award of ecolabels for environmentally less damaging products. In the UK the scheme is administered by the United Kingdom Ecolabelling Board. This will judge various competing products, and award ecolabels to those which are shown to be environmentally less damaging than alternatives.

### How?

#### The ecolabel

The ecolabel scheme grants awards to environmentally less damaging products. This could affect your purchasing strategy. Since the Ecolabelling Board will assess all aspects of a product's manufacture, use and disposal, you may have to consider the raw materials and intermediate products used in its manufacture if the final product is to get the ecolabel.

### Further information

Turn to the Environmental policy topic at p. 185 in Volume 2 for more detailed coverage of this measure.

# 2.9 Information technologies and telecommunications

## Are you affected?
You are affected if:
- you are responsible for purchasing your company's telecommunications services and equipment;
- you use electronic date interchange (EDI) as a means of communicating with your suppliers;
- some form of electronic link-up with your suppliers would be helpful in speeding up and making more accurate the purchasing function within your company;
- you are responsible for purchasing within a telecommunications utility.

## Why?
- The Commission's telecommunications programme has as its aim the liberalisation of the market for telecommunications services and equipment. This should mean wider choice at lower cost for you as a consumer. Although the UK market is already liberalised relative to member states, the entry of non-UK competitors into the market should intensify competition further.

  In addition to this, the Community's proposals for telecommunications services include the concept of a single point of contact for purchasing telecommunications services on a community-wide basis.
- The Commission is funding two programmes aimed at promoting the development of new kinds of information services. One is the Trade Electronic Data Interchange Systems (TEDIS) programme which promotes electronic data interchange (EDI – the exchange of data between computer systems) throughout the EC and EFTA countries.

  The second is called IMPACT – Information Market Policy Actions. It aims to promote the single market for electronic information services, and includes actions to overcome legal and administrative barriers, increase user-friendliness, improve information literacy, and support information initiatives. Both programmes operate through calls for proposals for collaborative projects.
- EDI could be an important medium for you to use in communicating with your suppliers more speedily and accurately, if you do not use it already.
- Purchasing by a telecommunications utility may now be subject to the new EC procurement rules, irrespective of whether the utility is publicly or privately owned. See Chapter 11 of Volume 2 for more information about how to comply with these rules.

## How?

The main ways in which the purchasing function will be affected by EC information technologies and telecommunications policy are:

### Overhead costs

The liberalisation of the market for telecommunications services and equipment should ensure a wider choice of these products at lower cost for you as a consumer. This means that you may be able to take advantage of better and more cost-effective deals in the future, and thus you may wish to monitor the developments in telecommunications liberalisation. This may be of even greater relevance if your company uses telecommunications services heavily, for example within logistics, operations or sales. Such services could include fax, networks, data and the value-added services or, in the UK, voice telephony. However, voice telephony in the rest of Europe is not subject to competition at the moment.

A single point of contact for negotiating Community-wide telecommunications services contracts may cut some of your costs as duplication is avoided. However, this is a relatively long-term plan, considering the problems still to be overcome regarding an open market in all aspects of telecommunications services and equipment.

### EDI and other information services

Information services, including EDI, enable suppliers and customers to exchange orders and process documentation directly and automatically via their computers. This may be useful to your purchasing function by making the process quicker and more accurate.

However, the freer exchange of information generally, and easier access to customers, suppliers and so on, depends upon the harmonisation of telecommunications and other electronics standards, which is part of an ongoing process.

## Further information

Turn to the Information technologies and telecommunications topic at p. 239 in Volume 2 for more detailed coverage of these measures.

## 2.10 Financial services

### Are you affected?
Your business is affected if:
- you purchase banking products and services;
- you purchase investment services.

### Why?
- Community legislation covering financial services providers within the Community is likely to lead to a general increase in:
  * the number of firms offering 'pan-Community' financial products and services;
  * the range of financial products and services aimed at the corporate client;
  * the value and quality of services offered.
- Community legislation covering investment will increase your choice of products and banking and investment services on offer both within the UK and from other member states.

### How?
The main ways in which the purchasing function will be affected by EC financial services policy measures are:

#### The opening up of the banking sector
The second banking co-ordination Directive allows credit institutions (broadly speaking, banks and building societies) and certain of their subsidiaries to establish a branch in, or provide a broad range of banking and financial services to any member state on the basis of their home EC state authorisation – through the mechanism of the so-called 'single passport' – or banking license.

For institutions to receive this passport, they must meet minimum standards of authorisation and supervision, laid down in the Directive.

While an increase in the number of credit institutions to which they have access will increase consumers' choice, it is likely that suppliers will generally compete on the quality of their services, rather than focusing on price.

#### The opening up of the investment services sector
The investment services Directive will allow investment firms (as defined) to establish a branch in, or provide a range of investment services in, any member state on the basis of their home EC state authorisation – a similar 'single passport' to that for banks. For firms to be eligible for this passport

they must comply with certain minimum standards of authorisation and supervision, laid down in the Directive.

The Directive also includes minimum standards for Community banks' and investment firms' access to membership of Community stock exchanges and other regulated securities markets.

Although it is unlikely that the number of investment services providers will increase significantly as a result of this legislation, the nature of their offerings may change to reflect the increasing importance of Community trade to UK companies.

## Further information

Turn to the Financial services topic at p. 299 in Volume 2 for more detailed coverage of these measures.

# 2.11 Insurance

## Are you affected?

Your business is affected if:

- you purchase non-life insurance;
- you purchase motor insurance;
- you purchase life assurance.

## Why?

- The second non-life insurance Directive (implemented in July 1990 in the UK) introduced arrangements under which an insurance company could sell non-life insurance (other than motor insurance) to customers in another member state on a services basis, that is, without having an establishment in that state after having notified the supervisory authorities of that state. The third non-life insurance Directive, adopted in June 1992, introduces a single-licence system, enabling insurance companies whose head office is situated in a member state to carry on non-life insurance business throughout the Community, subject only to a single authorisation granted by their home state authorities and notification to the supervisory authorities of each member state in which it is to sell insurance.

- A series of three Directives, the first, second and third motor insurance Directives, achieve a high degree of harmonisation of member states' laws on compulsory motor insurance. The motor insurance services Directive, implemented in the UK in November 1992, extends the regime introduced by the second non-life insurance Directive to motor insurance.

- The second life insurance Directive introduces the same regime as the second non-life insurance Directive but for life assurance (with the exclusion of pension fund management) and is due to be implemented by 21 May 1993. A further Directive, adopted in November 1992 (the third life assurance Directive), introduces a single licence system for companies selling life assurance and enables such companies with head offices in member states to carry on life insurance business throughout the Community subject only to a single authorisation granted by their home state authorities and notification to the authorities of the member states in which the policies are to be sold.

These Directives should open up the Community market for insurance products and increase the pressure on insurers to offer high value and quality insurance products.

## How?

The main ways in which the purchasing function will be affected by insurance measures are:

### Increased choice of non-life insurance products

The second non-life insurance Directive provides a regulatory framework within which most non-life risks may be covered on a cross-frontier basis.

The third non-life insurance Directive will provide a single licence system for non-life insurance. Under the single licence, insurers with a head office in any member state will be able to provide direct non-life insurance throughout the Community on the strength of its home state authorisation.

Despite the potential increase in competition resulting from this opening up of the Community market, it is unlikely that premiums offered by new entrants will be significantly cheaper than those offered already by companies in the UK. On the other hand, companies needing to insure risks in several member states should find it easier to obtain competitively priced cover matched to their needs, and should be able to cover such risks within a single policy if they so wish.

### Increased choice of motor insurance products

The motor insurance services Directive enables an insurer in one member state to cover motor liability risks in any other member state without needing to have a branch or subsidiary there.

The first, second and third motor insurance Directives achieve a high degree of harmonisation of member states' laws on compulsory motor insurance, to protect the parties insured and road accident victims.

The UK motor insurance market is already highly price competitive, but companies whose employees travel in other member states should benefit, since policies automatically provide third-party cover throughout the EC.

### Increased choice of life assurance products

Both the second and third life assurance Directives are aimed at opening up the Community market for life assurance products. The third life assurance Directive extensively modifies the regimes created by previous Directives by introducing a single-licence system. An insurer with a head office in any member state will be able to provide life assurance anywhere in the Community either on a cross-frontier basis, or through local establishment on the strength of its home state authorisation.

Although this should increase choice for purchasers of life assurance, you may not see many cost benefits as the UK market is already among the most liberalised in the Community, and is highly price competitive.

## Further information

Turn to the Insurance topic at p. 319 in Volume 2 for more detailed coverage of these measures.

# 2.12 Food law

## Are you affected?

Your business is affected if:

- you purchase fresh or processed foods for resale within the UK or the Community.

## Why?

Framework Directives are now in place covering materials in contact with food, labelling, presentation and advertising, foods for particular nutritional uses, additives and flavourings, the official control of foodstuffs, hygiene of foodstuffs and contaminants in food.

## How?

The main ways in which the purchasing function will be affected by food law are:

### Materials in contact with food

This legislation, in force in the UK since 1987, is aimed at minimising any health risk to consumers from contamination of food by substances transferring from the materials in contact with it. Both pre-packed and loose foods should only come into contact with materials manufactured in accordance with this legislation.

### Labelling, presentation and advertising

This Directive, fully in force in the UK since 1984, sets out standard rules relating to the labelling, presentation and advertising of foodstuffs for sale to the ultimate consumer and includes quantity marking provisions. The rules have since been extended to require alcoholic strength marking, to harmonise date marking, and to require labelling to indicate if a food has undergone irradiation. Rules for nutrition labelling will come into effect fully on 1 October 1993, but may be observed now. Detailed controls on nutrition and other claims that manufacturers may make about their products have yet to be negotiated. Meanwhile national rules continue to apply.

### Foods for particular nutritional uses

This Directive, adopted in May 1989, covers infant and follow-on formulae, baby foods, low-energy foods, dietary foods for special medical purposes, low-sodium foods, gluten-free foods, foods for sports people and diabetic foods. Regulations made under the Food Safety Act 1990 will be in force in Great Britain in 1993. Similar arrangements will apply in Northern Ireland.

The Directive includes consumer protection clauses relating to the claims manufacturers can make about the properties of their products.

### Food additives and flavourings

These Directives, in force in the UK since September 1992, lay down the general safety and labelling requirements for food additives and flavourings sold at wholesale and retail level. All additives and flavourings should comply with the requirements of this legislation.

### The official control of foodstuffs

This Directive, in force in the UK since 1991, provides for member states to carry out inspections at all stages of the manufacturing and distribution chain to ensure that Community food law is complied with.

The same rules apply to food for export to other member states and third countries.

### Contaminants in food

A common position has been reached on this proposal Regulation which lays down a procedure for setting limits on contaminants in foods. Subsequent measures on specific contaminants will be proposed by the Commission. Contaminants which are the subject of more specific Community rules, such as pesticides and veterinary medicines, are not covered by this Regulation.

### Hygiene of foodstuffs

A common position has been reached on this proposed Directive which would establish general hygiene principles to be followed by all food businesses. It would cover production, through to sale, of foodstuffs to the final consumer. The provisions of the Directive are broadly similar to existing requirements of UK law.

## Further information

Turn to the Food law topic at p. 373 in Volume 2 for more detailed coverage of these measures and proposals.

## 2.13 Pharmaceuticals

### Are you affected?

Your business is affected if:

- you purchase medicinal products for human use in other member states.

### Why?

Disparities in national pricing systems for medicines could affect intra-Community trade if they were operated so as to favour (or disadvantage) certain manufacturers. In order to remove barriers to trade, and thus stimulate free competition, the Community has agreed standards of transparency for national pricing systems. In particular, decisions should be taken on the basis of objective and verifiable criteria.

This measure should eliminate discrimination in the member states and provide you with a wider choice of suppliers across the Community.

### How?

Transparency of pricing measures in the Community will make it more difficult for one member state's national authorities to put products from another member state at a disadvantage by delaying decisions on price applications, and awarding them uncompetitive prices. This should eliminate discrimination and increase competition thus enabling you to consider new sources of supply.

Greater transparency and increased competition is likely to lead to a convergence of price levels across the Community.

### Further information

Turn to the Pharmaceuticals topic at p. 381 in Volume 2 for more detailed coverage of this measure.

# 3 · The **OPERATIONS AND LOGISTICS** function

| 3.1 | **Transport** | 77 |
| 3.2 | **Standards** | 79 |
| 3.3 | **Excise duties** | 81 |
| 3.4 | **Frontier controls** | 83 |
| 3.5 | **Trade policy and customs duties** | 84 |
| 3.6 | **Freedom of movement for workers** | 85 |
| 3.7 | **Employment** | 87 |
| 3.8 | **Health and safety** | 89 |
| 3.9 | **Energy policy** | 93 |
| 3.10 | **Environmental policy** | 94 |
| 3.11 | **Competition policy** | 96 |
| 3.12 | **Food law** | 98 |
| 3.13 | **Pharmaceuticals** | 100 |

# 3.1 Transport

## Are you affected?

Your business is affected if:

- you operate your own freight transport fleet.

## Why?

The large numbers of regulatory changes and reductions in transport times and costs brought about by Community legislation could reduce the financial benefits of operating your own distribution fleet.

## How?

The main ways in which the operations and logistics function may be affected by EC transport measures are:

### Regulatory changes

Businesses operating their own road haulage fleet will be affected by a number of new and proposed Community laws and resolutions covering:

- driver training;
- taxation;
- vehicle specifications.

Fleets must comply with these laws if they are to continue operating in the domestic market, or start to access other member state markets.

### The reduced costs of transport services

The liberalisation of the Community's transport industries, brought about by EC legislation, is likely to lead to:

- increased competition in the different transport industries;
- a downward pressure on margins; and
- some industry restructuring, with a potential increase of concentration within the UK industry.

You may need to reassess the financial benefit of operating an in-house distribution fleet, since it may become more cost and time efficient for a third party to provide this service. Options might include:

- buying in your distribution needs; and
- offering your distribution services to other businesses as well as your own – that is, competing as a freight transporter.

## Further information

Turn to the Transport topic at p. 27 in Volume 2 for more detailed coverage of these measures.

# 3.2 Standards

## Are you affected?

Your business is affected if:

- your products conform to a national or European standard underpinning a regulation; you are, or you have been, affected by technical regulations concerning, for example, product safety, environmental issues, quality or consumer protection;
- as a provider of goods or services, your processes or systems could be considered to be of a high standard;
- you have had to have your product tested many times in order for it to be allowed into other member states.

## Why?

- If your product is covered by one of the Community's technical standards Directives, whether it is an old or a New Approach measure, it must conform to the technical details or essential requirements as outlined in the Directive so that it can be sold in the EC. This is true whether or not the product is traded across borders. A limited number of products are covered by these Directives.
- BS 5750 is a standard recognising quality management systems or processes, identical to the international ISO9000 standard and the European standard EN29000. Attaining the standard creates confidence with clients that products will conform consistently to a standard or specification. It may also help you to cut costs by reducing waste and reworking.
- The Commission is aiming to reduce the need for multiple testing and certification by establishing mutual recognition of testing and certification bodies, for products covered by European technical regulations.

## How?

The main ways in which the operations and logistics function will be affected by EC standards measures are:

### Conforming to technical requirements

It is very important that you establish whether or not your product is covered by an old or New Approach Directive, and that, if it is covered, it conforms to that Directive. If, for any reason, your product does not conform to the technical details or essential requirements outlined in the Directive, you will not be allowed to sell it anywhere in the Community, regardless of whether or not it is traded across borders. The easiest way of ensuring that your product meets the requirements of the Directive is to ensure that it conforms to the national standard implementing a specified European standard. New Approach Directives are underpinned by European standards prepared by European standards bodies, usually CEN or CENELEC. They are then implemented as identically worded national standards.

Where no European legislation exists, the general principles is that if a product is fit to be sold in one member state, it is fit to be sold in any other – that is, there is mutual recognition by member states of each other's national regulations pending the development of measures outlining 'essential requirements'.

### BS 5750

BS 5750 lists the key requirements of a quality management system, which can be applied to almost any type of organisation. They include the need to establish a quality policy, to allocate responsibility clearly, to give authority to those allocated responsibility, to document each stage of the production process, and to establish systems for identifying, remedying and preventing defects in quality.

### Multiple testing in the non-regulated field

If your product is tested in a laboratory or certified by a body which applies and is nationally accredited to European standard criteria (the EN45000 series), it is likely that, at some point in the future, it may not need rechecking. This will save you both time and money. If you have decided not to sell in Europe because of this barrier, you may wish to explore this option again.

The European Organisation for Testing and Certification (EOTC) has been set up to encourage the development of mutual recognition agreements. It is an autonomous unit in which participation by interested parties is on a purely voluntary basis. You may wish to become involved in the EOTC, and take advantage of the facility that it provides.

## Further information

Turn to the Standards topic at p. 13 in Volume 2 for more detailed coverage of these measures.

# 3.3 Excise duties

## Are you affected?

Your business is affected if:

- you transport excisable goods across frontiers between member states.

## Why?

- New rules have been agreed for the transport and storage of duty-suspended goods (goods 'in bond') with which you have to comply.
- The minimum rates for leaded and unleaded petrol, and diesel may affect the price of these fuels in different member states.

## How?

The main ways in which the operations and logistics function are affected by EC excise duties policy are:

### Transport and storage of duty-suspended goods

Community legislation means that since 1 January 1993 movement of duty-suspended goods subject to excise duty takes place between authorised warehouse keepers or registered traders in another member state. Authorised warehouse keepers are able to produce, hold, receive and despatch excisable goods while duty suspended. Registered traders (known as 'registered excise dealers and shippers' in the UK) are only able to receive duty-suspended goods from another member state and the duty must be paid on receipt of the goods. (They are not be able to hold duty-suspended goods.) Both authorised warehouse keepers and registered traders must be registered in their member state. In addition, non-authorised traders are able to make occasional purchases of duty-suspended goods from authorised warehouse keepers in another member state, provided that payment of the excise duty is guaranteed prior to the despatch of the goods.

The legislation aims to monitor and control the movement of goods by means of an accompanying document. A full set of commercial documentation (or approved documents) has to accompany each consignment, including details of goods, mode of transport, despatching and receiving parties, consignment number and estimated time for the journey.

### Fuel oils

The agreement to impose a harmonised structure and the agreed minimum rate of duty on leaded and unleaded petrol and diesel may affect the relative prices of these fuels in different member states (but not in the UK).

## 82 • THE **OPERATIONS AND LOGISTICS** FUNCTION

**Further information**

Turn to the Excise duties topic at p. 63 in Volume 2 for more detailed coverage of these measures.

## 3.4 Frontier controls

### Are you affected?
Your business is affected if:
- you distribute products across internal borders in the Community.

### Why?
As well as benefiting from efforts to improve transportation within the Community (see Chapter 3, Transport in Volume 2), Community firms are likely to be benefiting from the removal on 1 January 1993 of controls which existed at internal borders. This should give firms the opportunity to improve the efficiency of their product distribution and to consider supplying more geographically distant customers, as transport costs and delays caused by controls decrease.

### How?
The main way in which the operations and logistics function is affected by frontier controls measures is:

**Reduced costs and transportation times**
The overall objective of the Community's frontier controls legislation is to abolish restrictions on the free movement of goods between member states. To facilitate this, the Community drew up a two-stage system, the first stage being effective from 1 January 1988.

The key element of the first stage was that all member states would recognise a single administrative document (SAD) for customs clearance purposes. This simplified the paperwork involved in transporting goods between member states. Previously, as many as 70 different forms needed to be completed.

Stage two involved the co-ordination of policies and the adoption of common legislation to allow the complete elimination of internal frontiers and controls on the movement of goods within the EC, including the SAD, by 1 January 1993.

These initiatives, combined with the improvements under way in the Community's transport industries, are likely to lead to transport costs being reduced by up to 5 per cent and transport times being reduced by up to 30 per cent depending on routes taken (see Chapter 3 (Transport) of Volume 2).

### Further information
Turn to the Frontier controls topic at p. 69 in Volume 2 for more detailed coverage of this measure.

# 3.5 Trade policy and customs duties

## Are you affected?

Your business is affected if:

- you import or export goods between the Community and members of the European Free Trade Association (EFTA);
- you import goods from outside the Community.

## Why?

- Further changes are being made to the Community's customs procedures to take account of changes resulting from the completion of the single market, to harmonise the member states' customs procedures.
- As the Community progresses towards a single market, detailed changes are being made to customs formalities to harmonise member states' customs procedures affecting goods imported from outside the Community once they are in free circulation within the Community.

## How?

The main way in which the operations and logistics function will be affected by EC trade and customs duties policy is:

### Customs formalities

Detailed changes are being made to customs formalities to take account of the changes resulting from the completion of the internal market. The changes cover customs warehouses and free zones, release of goods into free circulation, responsibilities of importers, and temporary importation.

### Inward and outward processing

Inward and outward processing rules may allow you to process imports in the Community and re-export them or have Community goods processed in third countries and re-import them under advantageous tariff rules. Regulations specify the conditions under which this can be done.

## Further information

Turn to the Trade and customs duty topic at p. 79 in Volume 2 for more detailed coverage of these measures and how far they are extended to the EFTA countries.

# 3.6 Freedom of movement for workers

## Are you affected?
Your business is affected if:
- you provide professional services in more than one member state;
- recruitment is the principal business of your company;
- training is the principal business of your company.

## Why?
In order to complete the single market, and, in particular, to eliminate remaining obstacles to freedom of movement for workers, the Community is seeking to ensure the recognition of professional qualifications, that is, the right for fully qualified professionals from one member state to join their profession and practise in another member state. This should make it easier for professional staff to be deployed from one member state to another.

## How?
The main ways in which the operations and logistics function will be affected by freedom of movement for workers are:

### Professional services
The first general Directive on higher education diplomas sets out a system for 'mutual recognition' of professional qualifications which require at least three years' degree-level study. It applies to professions which are directly or indirectly regulated by the state, including professions regulated by chartered bodies. This new system should make it easier for you to be authorised by the corresponding professional body in another member state in order to set up business and to provide services to business or personal customers throughout the Community. However, you should also be aware that you may be facing greater competition in the UK market, as access to the latter is likely to be attractive to potential competitors from other member states.

### Recruitment
If recruitment is the basis of your business, the pool of professionals from which you recruit will widen as you will be able to approach and consider candidates from other member states.

### Training

If training is the basis of your business, there will be opportunities for you to help would-be migrants – either UK nationals wanting to go to another member state or other Community nationals wanting to come in the UK – to make up for gaps in their own training.

## Further information

Turn to the Freedom of movement for workers topic at p. 89 in Volume 2 for more detailed coverage of these measures.

# 3.7 Employment

## Are you affected?

Your business is affected if:

- you employ part-time or temporary staff;
- the effective scheduling of work is important to your operations;
- you post workers to other member states temporarily to provide services there, or you are a user of such temporary labour from other member states;
- you employ young people under 18 years of age.

## Why?

- Proposals regarding part-time and temporary workers whose average weekly working time is at least eight hours a week would ensure that such staff would be treated in the same way as full-time staff on a pro-rata basis. Part-time and temporary workers would be eligible for the benefits covered by the Directives, which concern the majority of those benefits which are available to full-time staff. This may increase your employment costs.
- The terms and conditions of employment for employees are under scrutiny in a Commission proposal which aims to set out the work and rest periods for staff. If passed, this could increase your labour costs, and also affect the flexibility of your operations.
- A proposal could effect the employment terms and conditions of workers posted into a member state in the framework of the provision of services. It would apply to workers posted as part of a contract or by temporary employment businesses and would also include postings within firms or groups of firms.
- A proposed Directive would regulate young people's hours of work and could prevent their employment in certain activities.

## How?

The main ways in which the operations and logistics function will be affected by EC employment policy are:

### Part-time and temporary workers

The Commission proposals would ensure that part-time workers working eight hours a week or longer and in some cases, temporary workers, be treated the same way as full-time permanent employees for entitlement to certain statutory rights and occupational benefits. Part-time and temporary employees would be entitled, on a pro-rata basis, to vocational training, holidays, dismissal and seniority allowances and protection under statutory and occupational social security schemes.

### Working time

The Commission proposal as amended by discussion amongst member states:

- sets daily and weekly rest periods;
- sets paid annual holiday entitlements;
- limits the working week to 48 hours but member states have the choice of allowing workers to work longer voluntarily;
- places some restrictions on night work.

### Posted workers

Commission proposals would require member states to ensure that posted workers are not deprived of the benefit of relevant rules or legally binding agreements in areas such as pay and working hours that apply in the member state to which they are posted. The relevant rules and agreements include those relating to pay, paid holiday, hours, health and safety, hiring conditions, maternity leave and equal treatment. There is a three-month threshold on the application of pay and holiday rules to postings.

### Employment of young people

On the basis of the current proposals the Directive would impose restrictions on the employment of young people. Employers would have to:

- restrict working time, and would need to specify daily, weekly and annual rest periods for those under 18 years old;
- conduct a risk assessment of jobs where young people are likely to be exposed to certain hazards;
- provide alternative jobs where risks have been identified; and
- require medical surveillance of young people.

In certain circumstances there would be limitations on deploying young people in certain types of jobs. There could be sanctions for failing to comply with the provisions of the Directive. The overall effect, if the Directive is not modified in the course of negotiations, could lead to less flexibility in deploying and training young people.

## Further information

Turn to the Employment topic at p. 105 in Volume 2 for more detailed coverage of these measures and proposals.

# 3.8 Health and safety

## Are you affected?

You are affected if:

- you are responsible for your work premises;
- you employ staff.

## Why?

- Community legislation on health and safety in the workplace is becoming increasingly wide-ranging and detailed. To address it effectively in future years, it may have to become a greater managerial priority for many Community firms. Many firms will incur increased direct costs as:

  ★ they are required to comply with Community legislation immediately it comes into force in each member state;

  ★ they spend more managerial and staff time on health and safety matters.

## How?

The main ways in which the operations and logistics function may be affected by EC health and safety measures are:

### Safer workplaces

The workplace Directive lays down general health and safety criteria for workplaces in existence at the end of 1992, and for those established after that date. Most of these requirements were already covered by UK law, but firms will need to ensure that premises have:

- adequate welfare facilities;
- adequate ventilation;
- sufficient and suitable lighting;
- rest rooms where necessary;
- facilities for pregnant women and nursing mothers to rest when necessary;
- safeguards against injury from falls or falling objects; and
- facilities for handicapped staff.

'Existing' workplaces have until 31 December 1995 to comply. Workplaces used for the first time after 1 January 1993, or modified after that date, will have to comply at once.

## Industry-specific health and safety requirements

The safety framework Directive also laid the groundwork for the introduction of individual Directives to deal with certain industrial sectors, substances and workplace environments. Some of these Directives – for example, the workplace and work equipment Directives – refine previous UK law, whereas others deal with very specific situations which are only partially covered by pre-1975 legislation, such as the draft proposal on medical assistance on board ships, or the Directive on exposure to biological agents.

The Directives are specific, detailed and numerous, and, as the number is constantly increasing, it is important that firms realise the considerable effort that must go into:

- monitoring continuous developments;
- achieving compliance with the relevant legislation.

## Increased use of safety signs

The safety signs Directive (adopted 24 June 1992) requires employers to use safety signs wherever their employees are exposed to a danger or risk which has not been eliminated or adequately controlled by using normal health and safety procedures.

It applies to all premises under the control of the employer and activities where workers are employed, but excludes signs used in connection with the transportation of dangerous substances.

It extends the meaning of safety signs to include other forms of communication, such as hand signals, acoustic signals and illuminated signs.

The Directive must be implemented by 24 June 1994.

## Updating display-screen equipment

The display-screen equipment Directive obliges employers to evaluate the health and safety risks of workstations which contain display screens, and take steps to remedy such risks.

By 1996, workstations existing prior to 1 January 1993 will have to meet certain minimum requirements with regard to:

- design;
- environmental factors such as glare, lighting, humidity and noise; and
- design of the tasks to be performed and the software used.

Firms using display-screen equipment will be required to:

- ensure that the workstations meet the required standards;
- ensure display-screen workers have their work periodically interrupted by changes of activity or breaks;
- ensure display-screen workers receive regular eye tests; and
- provide information and training for workers.

New workstations put into service on or after 1 January 1993 will have to comply immediately with the requirements.

## HEALTH AND SAFETY · 91

The term 'display-screen equipment' covers screens of various types, and includes (but is not limited to) VDUs in offices.

### Reducing the manual handling of loads

The Directive on the manual handling of loads obliges employers to reduce the risk of injury by taking steps to avoid (or, where manual handling cannot be avoided, to reduce) the need for employees to move, lift or carry loads manually.

The risk of injury is not simply brought about by the weight of a load, but by its size and shape, and the conditions in which it is carried (for example, across uneven surfaces).

Complying with the Directive is likely to have cost implications as it will be necessary for firms to:

- assess their manual handling operations;
- introduce mechanical equipment in order to cope with heavy or bulky loads; and
- reorganise tasks or work areas in a such a way to reduce the risk to employees.

The provisions of the Directive will come into force in January 1993.

### The use of dangerous substances

A number of proposed and adopted Directives seek to make rules on the application of 'dangerous substances' in the workplace more stringent. This has implications for the cost of:

- monitoring and assessing the risks of such substances;
- replacing dangerous substances with less harmful ones;
- taking preventive action;
- consulting, informing, and training workers.

The term 'dangerous substances' covers a range of substances for which the Community has laid down statutory requirements relating to their use. Directives have been adopted or proposed on the following substances:

- carcinogens;
- biological, physical and chemical agents;
- asbestos;
- metallic lead and ionic compounds;
- benzene;
- pesticides;
- cadmium compounds;
- radioactive substances;
- explosive substances.

The requirements are specific, detailed and numerous, and, although a large number of Directives are already in place, they are continuously being added to and updated.

## Further information

Turn to the Health and safety topic at p. 125 in Volume 2 for more detailed coverage of these measures and proposals.

## 3.9 Energy

### Are you affected?
Your business is affected if:

- you use significant quantities of energy.

### Why?
An Energy Council Decision to introduce the SAVE programme provides the framework for the introduction of measures to promote energy efficiency. Agreement has already been reached on the introduction of minimum standards for the efficiency of hot water boilers and on appliance labelling. A budget is available to fund technical evaluations of alternative methods to promote energy efficiency.

### How?
The SAVE programme's measures will increase the information available regarding energy efficiency, by introducing labelling of certain appliances and buildings and the setting of more rigorous efficiency standards. These measures will enable you to find out more about the way in which your energy costs could be reduced.

### Further information
Turn to the Energy topic at p. 175 in Volume 2 for more detailed coverage of this measure.

# 3.10 Environmental policy

## Are you affected?

Your business is affected if:

- you have plans for a development project which is likely to have signficant environmental effects and which requires planning permission or some other form of development consent;
- you need information on the environment to support operational decisions.

## Why?

- Developers must undertake an environmental assessment of certain types of projects which are likely to have significant effects on the environment by virtue of factors such as the nature of the development (for example, chemical plant, transport infrastructure, waste disposal installation, and so on), its size or its location. Developers must submit an environmental statement describing the project, discussing likely significant environmental effects and detailing measures to avoid or reduce any significant adverse effects with their application for planning permission or other form of development consent.
- A Directive allows the public greater freedom of access to information on the environment, held by certain public bodies with responsibilities for the environment, for example, data on air, water, soil, natural sites or other land, flora and fauna.

## How?

The main ways in which the operations and logistics function is affected by EC environmental policy are:

### Consent for new developments

The Directive on environmental assessment means that you now have to take the likely environmental effects of developments into account before undertaking certain types of new project. This may mean that you will have to consult widely on the environmental effects of your proposed development. You will have to prepare an environmental statement on these environmental effects to submit with your application for planning permission or other form of development consent. Environmental information will be taken into account by the relevant authority before a decision for the development is given. The requirements of the Directive may entail extra research and administrative costs, as well as affecting the timetable of the planning process.

### Access to information

Greater access to relevant information on the state of the environment will enable you to assess the effects of different policies and allow you to compare the environmental condition of different geographical areas, which may be useful in appraising new investment projects. The Directive has been implemented in Great Britain by the Environmental Information Regulations 1992 (SI 1992 No. 3240). The Regulations will provide access, subject to safeguards on confidentiality, to environmental information not currently held on public registers.

## Further information

Turn to the Environmental policy topic at p. 185 in Volume 2 for more detailed coverage of these measures.

# 3.11 Competition policy

## Are you affected?

Your business is affected if:
- you are involved, or intend to become involved, in a service franchise;
- you manufacture under licence.

## Why?

- Article 85 of the Treaty of Rome prohibits agreements between firms, decisions by associations of firms and concerted practices, which prevent, restrict or distort competition in the Community if trade between member states may be affected. Agreements meeting certain conditions may be exempted from the prohibition in Art. 85 and most agreements between small firms are not affected by the Community competition rules.
- The Community has adopted a block exemption Regulation which exempts some service franchise agreements from the rules contained in Art. 85. Service franchise agreements are licences granted by a franchisor and exploited by franchisees to provide services on premises of uniform appearance using the franchisor's business methods (see below for details).
- The Community has also adopted a block exemption Regulation which exempts some know-how licensing agreements from Art. 85. Know-how covers non-patented technical information such as descriptions of manufacturing processes, recipes, formulae and drawings (see below for details).

## How?

The main ways in which the operations and logistics function in your company will be affected by EC competition policy are:

### Service franchise

The franchise block exemption Regulation, which exempts some service franchise agreements from the prohibition in Art. 85, sets out the restrictions which may and those which may not be imposed on the franchisee or franchisors.

If you already have a franchise agreement, it is important to ensure that your agreement complies with the rules of the Regulation. The Commission can withdraw exemption from an agreement in certain circumstances, for example, when there is a lack of adequate competition. You may need to obtain specialist legal advice. You should be aware that if your agreement does not comply with the rules of the Regulation, it will, if it infringes Art. 85, be automatically void.

If you are a small organisation, many of the franchise agreements you conclude with similar sized companies will not be regarded as infringing Art. 85.

## Licensing

The know-how licensing block exemption Regulation sets out the restrictions which licensors may and those they may not impose on the licensee.

If you already manufacture under licence it is particularly important to ensure that your agreement complies with the Regulation. The Commission can withdraw exemption from an agreement in certain specified circumstances. You should be aware that if your agreement does not comply with the rules of the Regulation, it will, if it infringes Art. 85, be automatically void.

If you are a small organisation, many of the know-how agreements you conclude with a similar sized company will not be considered as infringing Art. 85.

# Further information

Turn to the Competition policy topic at p. 203 in Volume 2 for more detailed coverage of these measures.

# 3.12 Food law

## Are you affected?

Your business is affected if:

- you produce or package fresh or processed foods;
- you store or transport fresh produce;
- you handle foods for sale to the final consumer;
- you manufacture food additives or flavourings in the UK or elsewhere in the Community.

## Why?

- Framework Directives are now in place covering materials in contact with food, labelling, presentation and advertising, foods for particular nutritional uses, additives and flavourings, the official control of foodstuffs, hygiene of foodstuffs, and contaminants in food.

## How?

The main ways in which the operations and logistics function will be affected by EC food law are:

### Materials in contact with food
This legislation, in force in the UK since 1987, is aimed at minimising any health risks to consumers from contamination of food by substances transferring from the materials in contact with it. Both pre-packed and loose foods should only come into contact with materials manufactured in accordance with this legislation.

### Labelling, presentation and advertising
This Directive, fully in force in the UK since 1984, sets out standard rules relating to the labelling, presentation and advertising of foodstuffs for sale to the ultimate consumer and includes quantity marking provisions. The rules have since been extended to require alcoholic strength marking, to harmonise date marking, and to require labelling to indicate if a food has undergone irradiation. Rules for nutrition labelling will take effect fully on 1 October 1993, but may be observed now. Detailed controls on nutrition and other claims that manufacturers may make about their products have yet to be negotiated. Meanwhile, national rules continue to apply.

### Foods for particular nutritional uses
This Directive, adopted in May 1989, covers infant and follow-on formulae, baby foods, low-energy foods, dietary foods for special medical purposes, low-sodium foods, gluten-free foods, foods for sports people and diabetic foods. Regulations made under the Food Safety Act 1990 will

be in force in Great Britain in 1993. Similar arrangements will apply in Northern Ireland.

The Directive includes consumer protection clauses relating to the claims manufacturers can make about the properties of their products.

### Food additives and flavourings

These Directives, in force in the UK since September 1992, lay down the general safety and labelling requirements for food additives and flavourings sold at wholesale and retail level. All additives and flavourings should comply with the requirements of this legislation.

### The official control of foodstuffs

This Directive, in force in the UK since 1991, provides for member states to carry out inspections at all stages of the manufacturing and distribution chain to ensure that Community food law is complied with.

The same rules apply to food for export to other member states and third countries.

### Contaminants in food

A common position has been reached on this Regulation which lays down a procedure for setting limits on contaminants in foods. Subsequent measures on specific contaminants will be proposed by the Commission. Contaminants which are the subject of more specific Community rules such as pesticides, veterinary medicines are not covered by this Regulation.

### Hygiene of foodstuffs

A common position has been reached on this proposed Directive which would establish general hygiene principles to be followed by all food businesses. It would cover production, through to sale, of foodstuffs to the final consumer. The provisions of the Directive are broadly similar to existing requirements of UK law.

## Further information

Turn to the Food law topic at p. 373 in Volume 2 for more detailed coverage of these measures and proposals.

# 3.13 Pharmaceuticals

## Are you affected?

Your business is affected if:

- you are a wholesale distributor of medicinal products for human or veterinary use;
- you manufacture medicinal products for human or veterinary use.

## Why?

To ensure the best conditions for the transport and handling of medicinal products, the Community has adopted Directives requiring wholesale distributors of such products to obtain special authorisations issued by member states' regulatory authorities. In order to obtain authorisation, wholesale distributors must satisfy a series of conditions, relating to, for example, record keeping, staff qualifications, and storage facilities.

In order to ensure that medicinal products are safe and of the right quality, the Community has adopted Directives which prescribe the conditions and circumstances in which such products may be manufactured. Manufacturers have to comply with detailed manufacturing requirements contained in the European Community Guide to Good Manufacturing Practice (GMP).

## How?

The main ways in which the operations and logistics function will be affected by pharmaceuticals measures are:

### Authorisation to distribute

As a wholesale distributor of medicinal products, you will need to apply for authorisation to the Medicines Control Agency at the Department of Health. The conditions which you will have to satisfy in order to obtain this authorisation are very similar to those already in existence in the UK under the licensing provisions of the Medicines Act 1968. However, if you do not at present require a licence (for example, if you are not selling such products) you may find that one will be required in future.

### Manufacturing practice

As a manufacturer of medicinal products, you must comply with the Directives that establish the principles and guidelines of good manufacturing practice. The Directives reflect, to a large extent, existing UK practice, and their impact on your activities is therefore unlikely to be substantial. You should be aware, however, that what was hitherto guidance or best practice is now subject to regulation.

## Further information

Turn to the Pharmaceuticals topic at p. 381 in Volume 2 for more detailed coverage of these measures.

# 4 · The **HUMAN RESOURCES** function

| | | |
|---|---|---|
| **4.1** | **Freedom of movement for workers** | 105 |
| **4.2** | **Employment** | 107 |
| **4.3** | **Health and safety** | 111 |
| **4.4** | **Company law** | 113 |
| **4.5** | **Structural funds** | 115 |

# 4.1 Freedom of movement for workers

## Are you affected?
- Do you feel that the pool of professionals from which you recruit is too small?
- Do you employ or provide training to nationals from other member states?

## Why?
- In order to complete the single market and in particular to eliminate remaining obstacles to the freedom of movement for workers, the Community is seeking to ensure the mutual recognition of professional and vocational qualifications, that is, the right for fully qualified professionals and for workers from one member state to be authorised by the corresponding professional bodies in another member state in order to practise and work there.
- Workers who are Community nationals, and their immediate families, already have the right to live and work anywhere in the Community. This right is also guaranteed for students enrolled on a vocational or professional training course.

## How?
The main ways in which the human resources function will be affected by the freedom of movement for workers are:

### Professional skills
The first general Directive on higher education diplomas sets out a system for 'mutual recognition' of professional qualifications which require at least three years' degree level study. It applies to professions which are regulated directly or indirectly by the state, including professions regulated by chartered bodies. The system will make it much easier for you to judge the suitability of applicants from other member states as they will have the opportunity to seek authorisation by the corresponding UK professional body before applying.

This will mean greater competition for UK professionals and greater opportunities for you to employ non-UK staff. However, it may also mean that some skills, already in short supply in the UK, may become scarce and professional staff more difficult to recruit, if UK workers decide to move to other member states.

### Right of residence

If you provide vocational or professional training you should be aware that a right of residence is granted to Community nationals enrolled on a vocational or professional training course, thus guaranteeing equal access to such training for all Community members. The right of residence also applies to Community nationals taking up employment anywhere in the Community.

## Further information

Turn to the Freedom of movement for workers topic at p. 89 in Volume 2 for more detailed coverage of these measures.

# 4.2 Employment

## Are you affected?

Your business is affected if:

- you are an employer;
- you determine employees' hours and patterns of work;
- you employ part-time or temporary staff;
- you employ women;
- you have operations in more than one member state, and employ more than 1,000 employees;
- you are likely to be making any employees redundant in the future;
- you post workers to other member states temporarily to provide services there or you are a user of such temporary labour from other member states;
- you employ young people under 18 years of age.

## Why?

- The Trade Union Reform and Employment Rights Bill 1992 contains provisions which translate into national legislation the terms of a Directive which requires that employees (who are employed to work eight hours a week and for an expected duration of one month or more) shall be entitled to a written statement of their main terms and conditions of employment. This statement will be required to be issued within two months of an employee's starting work or within two months of a written request from an existing employee.
- Commission proposals on working time could affect the hours and patterns of work and holiday entitlements of your employees.
- Proposals regarding part-time and temporary workers would mean that such staff would have to be treated in the same way as full-time staff. Part-time and temporary workers whose average weekly working time is at least eight hours a week would be eligible for many of the same benefits as other staff on a pro rata basis. This is likely to increase your costs of employment.
- A Directive adopted on 19 October 1992 gives all pregnant workers an entitlement to 14 weeks' maternity leave. It guarantees maintenance of all contractual rights, except for pay, during the leave and any absences from work for reasons of health and safety during pregnancy. Subject to qualifying conditions, during the period of the leave the worker must receive payment or an adequate allowance. Protection against dismissal from employment for reasons connected with pregnancy is also provided. The Directive must be implemented in UK law by

October 1994. The provisions to implement the employment protection aspects of the Directive are included in the Trade Union Reform and Employment Rights Bill 1992.
- Another proposed Directive, which the UK and other member states blocked in 1988, aimed to shift the burden of proof in sex discrimination cases. This would require the employer to prove that the person had not been discriminated against, as opposed to the current position, which places the burden of proof on the employee.
- Companies or groups of companies in Europe which operate in more than one member state and are above a specified size would, under another Commission proposal, be required to inform and consult with their employees via European Works Councils. These bodies, set up at the request of employees or their representatives, would act as representatives of the companies' employees and would have to be informed about any management proposal concerning the undertaking as a whole or at least affecting establishments in two member states, and likely to have serious consequences for the interests of employees.
- A Directive increases the amount of consultation you have with employee representatives before you make collective redundancies. It also closes up a loop-hole in the existing law by ensuring that companies take this law into account when making staff redundant in another country.
- A proposal could affect the employment terms and conditions of workers posted into a member state in the framework of the provision of services. It would apply to workers posted as part of a contract or by temporary employment businesses and would also include postings within firms or groups of firms.
- A proposed Directive would regulate young people's hours of work and could prevent their employment in certain activities.

## How?

The main ways in which the human resources function will be affected by EC employment policy are:

### Part-time and temporary workers

The Commission proposes to require that part-time workers are entitled to receive certain of the benefits of full-time workers on a pro-rata basis, if their average weekly working time is at least eight hours a week. Such benefits as vocational training, holidays, dismissal and seniority allowances and protection under statutory and occupational social security schemes would be affected. This would mean that the terms and conditions of employment for these staff may have to be revised and your overall labour costs may increase.

## Working time

The Commission proposal as amended by discussion amongst member states:

- sets daily and weekly rest periods;
- sets paid annual holiday entitlements;
- limits the working week to 48 hours but member states have the choice of allowing workers to work longer voluntarily;
- places some restrictions on night work.

## Conditions of employment

By June 1993, all member states will require employers to provide new recruits, who are employed to work more than eight hours a week and whose expected duration of employment exceeds one month, with a written statement of their main terms and conditions of employment. Existing employees must be given such a statement within two months of their making a written request.

## Pregnant workers

By October 1994, all member states must:

- require companies to provide women with 14 weeks' maternity leave, during which they would retain their contractual employment benefits except for pay. Subject to qualifying conditions, pay or an adequate allowance is to be provided for workers who are on maternity leave. The Directive will mean that the terms and conditions you offer to women may have to be revised. The Directive allows maternity pay to be funded by the employer, the State, or both;
- provide that the dismissal of a woman at any time from the beginning of her pregnancy up to the end of her maternity leave is automatically unfair, irrespective of her length of service or hours of work, unless it is for a reason unconnected with pregnancy or childbirth.

## Sex discrimination

Commission proposals would modify the burden of proof in sex discrimination cases so as to require changes to administrative and personnel procedures, introduce more documentation and might also increase the legal costs of fighting sex discrimination cases.

## European Works Councils

The Commission proposes to establish European Works Councils in large companies and groups of companies as a mechanism for informing and consulting with employees. The proposal would apply to:

- companies with a minimum of 1,000 employees in the Community and 100 employees in at least each of two member states;
- groups of companies with a minimum of 1,000 employees within the Community and at least two group undertakings in different member states each of which employs at least 100 employees within the Community.

The proposal, if adopted, would introduce a new tier of employee representation at European level.

### Collective redundancies

A new Directive increases the amount of consultation required before making collective redundancies. This could increase administrative costs.

### Posted workers

Commission proposals would require member states to ensure that posted workers are not deprived of the benefit of relevant rules or legally binding agreements in areas such as pay and working hours that apply in the member state to which they are posted. The relevant rules and agreements include those relating to pay, paid holidays, hours, health and safety, hiring conditions, maternity leave and equal treatment. There is a three-month threshold on the application of pay and holiday rules to postings.

### Employment of young people

On the basis of the current proposals the Directive would impose restrictions on the employment of young people. Employers would have to:

- restrict working time, and would need to specify daily, weekly and annual rest periods for those under 18 years of age;
- conduct a risk assessment of jobs where young people are likely to be exposed to certain hazards;
- provide alternative jobs where risks have been identified; and
- require medical surveillance of young people.

In certain circumstances there would be limitations on deploying young people in certain types of jobs. There could be sanctions for failing to comply with the provisions of the Directive. The overall effect, if the Directive is not modified in the course of negotiations, could lead to less flexibility in deploying and training young people.

## Further information

Turn to the Employment topic at p. 105 in Volume 2 for more detailed coverage of these measures and proposals.

## 4.3 Health and safety

### Are you affected?
Your business is affected if:
- you employ staff;
- you employ female staff;
- you employ temporary or part-time staff.

### Why?
- As health and safety legislation becomes an increasing managerial priority, employers may be required to appoint staff or advisors to manage health and safety activities.
- The Council has adopted a proposal for the protection at work of:
  * pregnant women;
  * women who have recently given birth;
  * women who are breast-feeding.

  Under the Directive (adopted on 19 October 1992, to be implemented by 19 October 1994), if the health of these employees is endangered in the workplace, Community employers either have to adjust their working hours and/or conditions, transfer them to alternative activities, or allow them to take leave on full pay.
  As well as the cost implications of this, Community firms may have to implement some organisational changes to ensure that women's responsibilities are covered by other workers or temporary staff.
- Under recent legislation, Community employers will be required to ensure that temporary or part-time staff enjoy the same level of health and safety protection as full-time employees.

### How?
The main ways in which the human resources function will be affected by health and safety measures are:

#### Requirements of employers
The basic demands by the Community on employers are outlined in the safety framework Directive, which was adopted in 1989. The responsibilities of employers include:
- assessing risks to employees and introducing preventive measures;
- developing a coherent overall health and safety policy;
- designating competent personnel to take charge of health and safety activities, or using outside services;

- providing health and safety information and training to workers;
- consulting with worker representatives on health and safety matters.

### Protection for pregnant women and recent mothers

The Directive for the protection at work of pregnant women, breast-feeding and recent mothers provides for the imposition of certain responsibilities on employers for the protection at work of the groups referred to. Employers will be required (using guidelines) to assess risks to health and safety which could arise from any of the non-exhaustive list of physical, biological and chemical agents, processes or working conditions given in the annexes to the Directive. If the assessment reveals a risk to employees' health or safety they must have their working conditions, hours, or job duties changed, or to be transferred to another activity. If such changes are not possible, they will be given leave for the whole of the period necessary to protect their safety or health.

### Increased rights for part-time staff

In order to meet new requirements for the health and safety of temporary and part-time staff, Community employers are likely to experience increased costs as they are required to:

- be responsible for the safety of workers supplied by employment agencies;
- provide relevant health and safety information to employment agencies;
- provide health and safety information and appropriate training to temporary employees;
- provide temporary staff with the same medical care as permanent workers;
- inform in-house health and safety personnel that temporary staff are employed there.

In addition, there is an optional provision in the Directive which would enable indvidual member states to ban temporary and part-time employees from certain types of dangerous work.

## Further information

Turn to the Health and safety topic at p. 125 in Volume 2 for more detailed coverage of these measures and proposals.

## 4.4 Company law

### Are you affected?
Your business is affected if:

- you are a limited liability company employing more than 1,000 employees.

### Why?
The Commission has introduced a number of legislative initiatives which relate to the involvement of employees in the businesses in which they work. These include the fifth Directive.

### How?
The main way in which the human resources function may be affected by company law is:

#### Compulsory employee participation
If you are a public limited company with over 1,000 employees, the current proposal for a fifth Directive, would, at the request of the majority of employees, make employee participation in a form prescribed by the Directive compulsory.

The worker participation provisions of the proposed fifth Directive do not take account of the voluntary system of employee involvement which exists in the UK.

### Further information
Turn to the Company law topic at p. 265 in Volume 2 for more detailed coverage of these proposals.

## 4.5 Structural funds

### Are you affected?
Your business could be affected if:
- you are likely to recruit the long-term unemployed or young people.

### Why?
The European Social Fund offers assistance to organisations which are financially supported by the public sector to improve the employment prospects of these workers by providing them with training opportunities and by stimulating the job market to help them find work. The European Coal and Steel Community also offers funds which can be used for retraining redundant coal and steel workers.

### How?

#### Employment and training grants
Some European Social Fund projects involve training based in the workplace, in local business. These measures aim to develop a better trained labour force by contributing to a greater level of vocational training activity. Assistance of this type is restricted in certain areas of the UK. You may wish to find out from the Department of Employment whether you are eligible.

### Further information
Turn to the Structural funds topic at p. 343 in Volume 2 for more detailed coverage of this measure.

# 5 · The **INFORMATION SYSTEMS** function

| | | |
|---|---|---|
| 5.1 | Intellectual property | 117 |
| 5.2 | Information technologies and telecommunications | 119 |

# 5.1 Intellectual property

## Are you affected?

Your business is affected if:

- you manufacture, supply or use computer programs, that is, software.

## Why?

The Community has sought to harmonise software copyright laws in the member states to ensure a common standard of protection for computer programs. The software Directive will ensure that computer programs are protected under copyright as literary works throughout the Community and that the unauthorised copying of a program is infringement of copyright in that program. Ideas and principles underlying a program, including those underlying its interface, are not protected.

## How?

The main ways in which the information systems function will be affected by EC intellectual property measures are:

### Manufacturers

The provisions of the software Directive closely mirrors existing law in the UK so that its impact on your activities as a manufacturer of software will not be substantial. However, the software Directive allows decompilation of a program without authorisation of the copyright owner to reproduce its code and translate its form in order to achieve interoperability of programs, that is, to make your program compatible with your competitors' products. This may enable you to enhance your product's performance.

The decompilation right is, however, strictly limited to achieving interoperability and must not be used for the development of a program substantially similar in its expression to that of the decompiled program. It is also allowed only where the information needed to achieve interoperability is not previously readily available.

### Users

As a lawful user of computer software you may reverse engineer (that is, analyse a program and decompile it, but only to the extent necessary to extract interface information) which may help you to make a program compatible with your existing systems. You may also correct program errors and make back-up copies.

This should provide you with greater access to the open systems market without running the risk of prosecution for piracy. Decompilation is only allowed, however, where it is indispensable for obtaining the necessary information for interoperability, and where the information is not previously readily available. The Copyright (Computer Programs)

Regulations 1992 implement the Directive, and you should study this to understand your rights as a lawful user.

When purchasing computer software, you should investigate the vendor's rights in the software, and, in particular, his right to assign or sub-licence any licensed software. You may otherwise run the risk of losing your status and rights as a 'lawful user' and may even incur liability as a 'secondary infringer'.

## Further information

Turn to the Intellectual property topic at p. 225 in Volume 2 for more detailed coverage of this measure.

# 5.2 Information technologies and telecommunications

## Are you affected?

You are affected if:

- you are responsible for maintaining your company's telecommunications and information systems.

## Why?

- You should be aware that the member states will introduce a single European number for emergency calls, 112, which may be used in parallel with any existing emergency number. A harmonised international access code, 00, is also being introduced.

## How?

The member states are introducing a single European emergency call number, 112, and a harmonised access code for international dialling, 00. In the UK, these will be introduced from 31 December 1992 and Easter 1995 respectively. 112 will operate in parallel with the existing 999 number.

## Further information

Turn to the Information technologies and telecommunications topic at p. 239 in Volume 2 for more detailed coverage of this measure.

# 6 · The RESEARCH AND PRODUCT DEVELOPMENT function

| | | |
|---|---|---|
| **6.1** | **Standards** | 123 |
| **6.2** | **Environmental policy** | 125 |
| **6.3** | **Intellectual property** | 126 |
| **6.4** | **Information technologies and telecommunications** | 127 |
| **6.5** | **Company law** | 129 |
| **6.6** | **Food law** | 130 |
| **6.7** | **Pharmaceuticals** | 132 |

# 6.1 Standards

## Are you affected?

Your business is affected if:

- your products conform to a national or European technical regulation or standard;
- you are, or have been, affected by technical regulations, concerned, for example, with product safety, environmental issues, quality or consumer protection;
- you have had to have your product tested many times in order for it to be allowed into other member states.

## Why?

- The Community is trying to prevent the establishment of new technical regulations which could constitute barriers to trade within the Community. Member states are required to notify the Commission in advance of new technical regulations relating to any industrial or agricultural product. Other member states may then object on the grounds that they constitute technical barriers to trade.

    If your product is covered by one of the Community's technical regulations or standards Directives, whether it is an 'old' or a New Approach measure, it must conform to the technical details or essential requirements as outlined in the Directive in order that it can be sold in the European Community. This holds whether or not the product is traded across borders.
- The Commission is aiming to end all mandatory multiple testing and certification requirements by establishing mutual recognition of testing and certification bodies, for products covered by European technical regulations.

## How?

The main ways in which the research and product development function will be affected by EC standards measures are:

### New standards and technical regulations as barriers to trade

New Approach Directives only outline the essential requirements that a product must meet in order to be sold in the Community. Although under Community law, member state authorities are required to accept on their market products which conform to the legislation and standards of other member states where these are intended to achieve equivalent objectives, the same principle of 'mutual recognition' cannot be applied to the individual purchaser in the market who is free to set his own requirements often by reference to national standards (not implementing European standards).

Alternatively, in the absence of a European standard, if you develop a product which conforms to a standard higher than that available in other member states, you can try to gain competitive advantage by pushing to establish your new standard as the basis for a new European standard through your trade association.

There are a number of ways in which you can keep abreast of developments in the creation of new draft technical regulations which might affect your product. The DTI circulates details of notified draft new technical regulations through various government departments to those most likely to be affected. Brief details are also published weekly by the Association of British Chambers of Commerce in 'Business Briefing'. They are also available on Spearhead, the DTI's single market database.

### Conforming to technical requirements

It is very important that you clarify whether your product is covered by an old or New Approach Directive, and that, if it is, it conforms to that Directive. If for any reason your product does not conform to the technical details or essential requirements outlined in the Directive, you will not be allowed to sell it anywhere in the Community, regardless of whether or not it is traded across frontiers. The easiest way of ensuring that your product meets the requirements of the Directive is to ensure that it conforms to the national standard implementing a specified European standard. New approach Directives are underpinned by European standards prepared by European standards bodies, usually CEN or CENELEC. They are then implemented as identically worded national standards.

Where no European legislation exists, the general principle is that if a product is fit to be sold in one member state, it is fit to be sold in any other – there is mutual recognition by member states of each other's national regulations pending the development of measures underpinning 'essential requirements'.

### Multiple testing

If your product is tested in a laboratory or certified by a body which applies and is nationally accredited to European standards criteria (the EN45000 series), it is likely that it will not need rechecking. This will save you both time and money.

The European Organisation for Testing and Certification (see p. 17 in Volume 2) has been set up to encourage the development of mutual recognition agreements. It is an autonomous unit in which participation by interested parties will be on a purely voluntary basis. You may wish to become involved in the EOTC, and take advantage of the facility that it provides.

## Further information

Turn to the Standards topic at p. 13 in Volume 2 for more detailed coverage of these measures.

# 6.2 Environmental policy

### Are you affected?

Your business is affected if:

- your new products are likely to be environmentally less damaging than alternatives.

### Why?

A Regulation from the EC sets out the procedures for the award of ecolabels for environmentally less damaging products. In the UK, the scheme is administered by the United Kingdom Ecolabelling Board. This will consider applications for the ecolabel against strict environmental criteria. It will award ecolabels to those products which are shown to be environmentally less damaging than alternatives.

### How?

The main way in which the research and product development function will be affected by environmental policy is:

#### The ecolabel

If you are developing a new product and you wish to take into account increased concern about the environment, you should seek advice from the United Kingdom Ecolabelling Board about the product groups which are covered by the scheme and the criteria that will be used to determine the awards of ecolabels.

### Further information

Turn to the Environmental policy topic at p. 185 in Volume 2 for more detailed coverage of this measure.

# 6.3 Intellectual property

## Are you affected?

Your business is affected if:

- you develop products or technologies for which you wish to obtain patents;
- you manufacture semiconductors.

## Why?

- In order to promote the free movement of goods and services, the Community is seeking to ensure the protection of patents on a Community-wide basis. The Community Patent Convention will make it possible to obtain a single patent valid in all member states.
- The Community has sought to harmonise member states' legislation on the protection of the design (topography) of the internal layout of semiconductor integrated circuits. A Directive, introduced in 1987, ensures the legal protection of topographies against unauthorised copying throughout the Community.

## How?

The main ways in which the research and product development function will be affected by EC intellectual property measures are:

### Community patent

The introduction of a single patent valid throughout the Community will mean that your products can be protected by a single patent covering all member states. The costs and inconvenience of maintaining separate patent registration in each member state will thus be eliminated.

### Semiconductors

As a semiconductor manufacturer, the Directive on the topographies of semiconductors will enable you to acquire protection for your product designs, thereby enabling you to recoup more research and development investment than at present.

## Further information

Turn to the Intellectual property topic at p. 225 in Volume 2 for more detailed coverage of these measures.

# 6.4 Information technologies and telecommunications

## Are you affected?

Your business is affected if:

- you use electronic data interchange (EDI) in product design, either between different departments within your company, or between your design department and one or more sub-contractors' design departments;
- some form of electronic link-up, either between different departments within your company, or between your design department and one or more sub-contractors' design departments, would be helpful in speeding up and making more accurate the sharing of product design information.

## Why?

- The Commission is funding two programmes aimed at promoting the development of new kinds of information services. One is the Trade Electronic Data Interchange Systems (TEDIS) programme which promotes electronic data interchange (EDI – the exchange of data between computer systems) throughout the EC and EFTA countries. The second is called Information Market Policy Actions (IMPACT). It aims to promote the single market for electronic information services, and includes actions to overcome legal and administrative barriers, increase user-friendliness, improve information literacy and support information initiatives. Both programmes operate through calls for proposals for collaborative projects.
- EDI could be an important medium for you to use in communicating product design information either within your company or between your design department and one or more of your sub-contractors' design departments more speedily and accurately, if you do not use it already.

## How?

The main way in which the research and product development function will be affected by EC information technologies and telecommunications policy is:

### EDI and other information services

Information services, including EDI, enable original equipment manufacturers and sub-contractors to exchange design and other product

# 128 • THE RESEARCH AND PRODUCT DEVELOPMENT FUNCTION

information directly and automatically via their computers. This may be useful to your research and product development function by making this process quicker and more accurate. However, the freer exchange of information generally, and easier access to customers, suppliers, and so on, depends upon the harmonisation of telecommunications and other electronics standards, which is part of an ongoing process.

## Further information

Turn to the Information technologies and telecommunications topic at p. 239 in Volume 2 for more detailed coverage of this measure.

# 6.5 Company law

## Are you affected?

Your business is affected if:

- you have links with firms in other member states which you wish to develop.

## Why?

The Community has created a framework for co-operation between businesses from different member states called the European Economic Interest Grouping (EEIG). The EEIG is designed to help companies, firms or individuals establish and maintain links with companies, firms or individuals in other member states.

## How?

The main way in which the research and product development function will be affected by company law is:

### Joint research and development

The European Economic Interest Group is a new form of business organisation aimed at providing a common framework for cross-border co-operation in certain activities.

A European Economic Interest Group could be used for joint research and development activities.

## Further information

Turn to the Company law topic at p. 265 in Volume 2 for more detailed coverage of this measure.

# 6.6 Food law

## Are you affected?

Your business is affected if:

- you carry out research and development into new food products.

## Why?

Framework Directives are now in place covering materials in contact with food, labelling, presentation and advertising, foods for particular nutritional uses, additives and flavourings, the official control of foodstuffs, hygiene of foodstuffs and contaminants in food.

## How?

The main ways in which the research and product development function will be affected by food law are:

### Materials in contact with food

This legislation, in force in the UK since 1987, is aimed at minimising any health risks to consumers from contamination of food by substances transferring from the materials in contact with it. Both pre-packed and loose foods should only come into contact with materials manufactured in accordance with this legislation.

### Labelling, presentation and advertising

This Directive, fully in force in the UK since 1984, sets out standard rules relating to the labelling, presentation and advertising of foodstuffs for sale to the ultimate consumer and includes quantity marking provisions. The rules have since been extended to require alcoholic strength marking, to harmonise date marking, and to require labelling to indicate if a food has undergone irradiation. Rules for nutrition labelling will take effect fully on 1 October 1993, but may be observed now. Detailed controls on nutrition and other claims that manufacturers may make about their products have yet to be negotiated, meanwhile national rules continue to apply.

### Foods for particular nutritional uses

This Directive, adopted in May 1989, covers infant and follow-on formulae, baby foods, low-energy foods, dietary foods for special medical purposes, low-sodium foods, gluten-free foods, foods for sports people and diabetic foods. Regulations made under the Food Safety Act 1990 will be in force in Great Britain in 1993. Similar arrangements will apply in Northern Ireland.

The Directive includes protection clauses relating to the claims manufacturers can make about the properties of their products. You should ensure that claims made for new products can be substantiated, and that the wording of those claims made on the packaging complies with the Directive.

### Food additives and flavourings

These Directives, in force in the UK since September 1992, lay down the general safety and labelling requirements for food additives and flavourings sold at wholesale and retail level. All additives and flavourings should comply with the requirements of this legislation.

### The official control of foodstuffs

This Directive, in force in the UK since 1991, provides for member states to carry out inspections at all stages of the manufacturing and distribution chain to ensure that Community food law is complied with.

The same rules apply to food for export to other member states and third countries.

### Contaminants in food

A common position has now been reached on this proposed Regulation which lays down a procedure for setting limits on contaminants in foods. Subsequent measures on specific contaminants will be proposed by the Commission. Contaminants which are the subject of more specific Community rules, such as pesticides, and veterinary medicines, are not covered by this Regulation.

### Hygiene of foodstuffs

A common position has been reached on this proposed Directive which would establish general hygiene principles to be followed by all food businesses. It would cover production, through to sale, of foodstuffs to the final consumer. The provisions of the Directive are broadly similar to existing requirements of UK law.

## Further information

Turn to the Food law topic at p. 373 in Volume 2 for more detailed coverage of these measures and proposals.

# 6.7 Pharmaceuticals

## Are you affected?

Your business is affected if:
- you develop new medicinal products for human or veterinary use which are likely to be marketed in more than one member state;
- the effective patent life of your products has been reduced because of delay occurred in obtaining market authorisation.

## Why?

- The Community's approach to intra-Community trade in medicinal products for human and veterinary use is currently based on a system of harmonised criteria for the assessment of licence applications. There are also procedures designed to help member states reach mutually agreed licensing decisions. However, member states often insist on reassessing products that have been licensed in another member state.

  The Council of Ministers has now reached agreement on a package of proposals, known as 'Future Systems', which, from around 1995, will begin to harmonise licensing decisions across the Community. There will be a centralised procedure for certain types of new medicines, such as those derived from biotechnology, whereby licensing decisions will be made by Community bodies and will be binding in all member states. For all other medicines (except homoeopathics), a decentralised procedure will operate, based on mutual recognition of national licensing decisions, with binding arbitration by Community bodies where member states disagree over a decision. The new procedures will be supported by a European Medicines Evaluation Agency (EMEA).

- The Community has agreed to allow firms to apply for a 'supplementary protection certificate' which provides an extension to the effective patent life of a product. This will compensate, in part at least, for the patent life lost in obtaining market authorisation for a new product. Your products are likely to benefit from this measure.

## How?

The main ways in which the research and product development function will be affected by Pharmaceuticals measures are:

### Product licences

If you develop and market certain biotechnology products or veterinary medicines intended for growth or yield promotion purposes, you will be required to apply to the EMEA for marketing authorisation under the centralised procedure when the Future Systems proposals come into operation.

Applications through this procedure will be optional for other biotechnology and innovative products.

The starting point for marketing authorisations for other medicinal products will be, as now, assessment by national licensing authorities. However, following a transitional period, once a licence has been granted in one member state, all applications to other member states will have to proceed through the decentralised procedure.

### Patent life

The 'supplementary protection certificate' restores to your patented medicinal products some of the patent term which is lost while a marketing authorisation is being obtained. The certificate gives most products an effective patent life of 15 years from the date at which it first begins to sell on the market, subject to the extension not being more than five years.

## Further information

Turn to the Pharmaceuticals topic at p. 381 in Volume 2 for more detailed coverage of these measures and proposals.

# 7 · The **FINANCE** function

| | | |
|---|---|---|
| **7.1** | **Free movement of goods, people, services and capital** | 137 |
| **7.2** | **VAT** | 138 |
| **7.3** | **Environmental policy** | 141 |
| **7.4** | **Intellectual property** | 142 |
| **7.5** | **Company law** | 143 |
| **7.6** | **Company taxation** | 145 |
| **7.7** | **Financial services** | 147 |
| **7.8** | **Insurance** | 149 |
| **7.9** | **Pharmaceuticals** | 151 |
| **7.10** | **Structural funds** | 153 |

# 7.1 Free movement of goods, people, services and capital

## Are you affected?

Your business is affected if:

- you wish to transfer capital or to invest in other member states;
- you are looking for new sources of funding in the Community.

## Why?

The Treaty of Rome recognised the free movement of capital within the Community as an essential complement to the free movement of goods, people and services. Progress on removing controls have varied between member states, but very few restrictions on capital movements now remain and only as derogations for a limited time for the less-favoured member states (Greece and Portugal). The Commission considers that full freedom of capital movements is necessary to ensure the creation of a single market in the financial services sector which will enhance competition and choice in financial services within the Community.

## How?

The main way in which the finance function may be affected by the free movement of capital is:

### Cross-border transfer and investment

Free movement of capital enables the transfer of funds across the Community and covers current transactions and capital investment.

Combined with the creation of a single market for financial services, it means access to more diverse and, possibly, cheaper sources of finance.

## Further information

Turn to the Free movement of goods, people, services and capital topic at p. 1 in Volume 2 for more detailed coverage of this measure.

# 7.2 VAT

## Are you affected?

Your business is affected if:

- your business is VAT-registered;
- you buy or sell goods or services which are liable for VAT from other member states;
- you sell goods by mail order;
- you entertain customers or clients;
- you provide company cars for employees;
- you are an exempt business or a non-taxable organisation which imports goods from other member states.

## Why?

VAT was one of the most contentious issues within the single market programme. Recently, agreement was reached on many important issues, for instance, the VAT rates Directive (92/77/EEC) which established a time-limited minimum standard rate of VAT and one or two optional reduced rates which member states may apply to an agreed list of goods and services. It also provided for the continuation of existing zero rates. Agreement was also reached on the administration of VAT after the abolition of frontier VAT controls.

Most of these agreements have already been translated into law. The finance function will need to adapt to the resulting changes in the structure, rates and administration of VAT. There may also be cash-flow implications for small to medium-sized enterprises. Whilst changes in rates in certain member states may affect demand for goods, all firms selling in that market should be affected equally.

## How?

The main ways in which the finance function is affected by EC VAT measures are:

### The destination and origin principles

From 1993 at least until the end of 1996, most cross-border commercial VAT transactions are based on the destination principle. This means that intra-Community sales are zero-rated by the seller, and VAT is paid by the VAT-registered customer at the rate in force in the country of consumption. It is intended that, after 1997, the origin principle will be introduced as the permanent solution to VAT collection, whereby VAT will be paid in the member state where the goods originate, at the VAT rate of that state.

## Cash flow

Smaller businesses will gain some cash flow benefits by paying VAT quarterly on intra-Community purchases. Businesses no longer have to pay VAT on goods at the time they are brought into the UK, but pay the VAT with their domestic quarterly VAT return. The UK government requires very large businesses (paying over £2m in VAT in the year ended March 1991) to pay their VAT monthly.

## Changes in rates

Some member states had to raise the level of VAT on certain products to bring them near to or in line with the agreed minimum standard rates, and this may reduce demand for certain products. The abolition of frontier controls leaves consumers free to shop cross-border, with certain exceptions such as new motorised land vehicles, boats and aircraft, and take advantage of lower tax rates in neighbouring member states. This may also affect regional sales for some products, but will depend on differences in VAT rates and access to products.

## EC sales lists

VAT-registered traders selling within the Community are required to provide the tax authorities with the VAT registration number and member state of their customers, and total supplies of goods to each customer on a quarterly basis. A new Regulation on administrative co-operation in the field of indirect taxation requires member states to exchange information from EC sales lists and to provide traders with the means of checking the VAT registration numbers of taxable persons in other member states. The purpose of these requirements is to prevent fraud.

## Trade statistics

All businesses have to provide the total value of supplies to and acquisitions from other member states on their VAT returns. Larger businesses with intra-EC arrivals or despatches above £135,000 per annum have to complete a more detailed monthly supplementary statistical declaration.

## Cross-border mail order

Detailed proposals for the management of VAT on cross-border distance selling transactions have been set down, which mean that the seller must set up a taxable presence in the relevant market if his sales in that member state exceed ECU 100,000 per annum, but most member states have opted for a lower threshold of ECU 35,000.

## Business expenses

The proposal on non-deductible business expenses, if it were adopted in its current form, would be likely to have most impact in the UK on the VAT currently reclaimed on company cars and employee subsistence payments. You may need to make changes in company policy regarding these. However, there is no consensus among member states on its operation, or when it should be introduced.

### Small and medium-sized enterprises

The UK government supports the move to ease the VAT burden on small and medium-sized enterprises. UK domestic reform has already gone some way towards this, and these proposals will not entail changes in the UK as radical as in some other member states (see Chapter 4 (VAT) in Volume 2).

## Further information

Turn to the VAT topic at p. 47 in Volume 2 for more detailed coverage of these measures and proposals.

# 7.3 Environmental policy

## Are you affected?

Your business is affected if:

- you are assessing proposals for projects which require planning permission or other forms of development consent.

## Why?

Projects which could significantly affect the environment may require environmental assessment as part of the planning permission or development consent process. Developers may have to submit a detailed environmental statement with their planning application.

## How?

The main way in which the finance function will be affected by environmental policy is:

### Consent for new developments

These requirements may affect your internal planning process as time and resources will need to be devoted to producing the environmental statement. Your criteria for assessing proposals for major capital expenditure projects may also be affected. In addition, where planning permission is required, the local planning authority has a maximum of 16 weeks in which to determine applications where an environmental statement has been submitted, rather than the usual eight weeks. This may lengthen the planning process and must therefore be taken into account when evaluating and costing the project.

## Further information

Turn to the Environmental policy topic at p. 185 in Volume 2 for more detailed coverage of this measure.

# 7.4 Intellectual property

## Are you affected?
Your business is affected if:
- you sell products or services for which you own patents or trade marks in other member states?

## Why?
In order to promote the free movement of goods and services, the Community is seeking to ensure the protection of patents and trade marks on a Community-wide basis.

The Community Patent Convention will make it possible to obtain a single patent valid in all member states, while the creation of a Community trade mark applicable in all member states will give a trade mark owner the exclusive right to use his mark throughout the Community. These measures should reduce the costs associated with multi-country patent and trade mark protection.

## How?
The main ways in which the finance function will be affected by EC intellectual property measures are:

### The Community patent
The introduction of a patent valid in all member states will eliminate the multiple procedures required to maintain a patent in each of the member states where an invention is to be sold.

Community patents will simplify renewal arrangements for patent protection in the Community. Moreover, the Convention will establish a system of law, common to all contracting states, to determine matters relating to infringement and validity of Community patents.

### Community trade mark
The creation of a Community trade mark issued by a single Community office (the Community Trade Mark Office) will eliminate the need to submit applications to trade mark authorities in the various countries in which the mark is to be used and should result in cost savings.

The Community trade mark will exist in parallel with national systems so if you seek only national coverage for your products or services, you can take the still cheaper option of applying solely for a national trade mark.

## Further information
Turn to the Intellectual property topic at p. 225 in Volume 2 for more detailed coverage of these measures.

## 7.5 Company law

### Are you affected?

Your business is affected if:

- you are a small or medium-sized firm;
- you have branches in other member states;
- you are a limited company involved in partnerships or unlimited companies in any member state;
- you are a partnership or an unlimited company and all your members with unlimited liability are limited companies.

### Why?

The Community company law programme aims to harmonise company law in different member states and hence to reduce costs associated with cross-border operations.

Recent measures include:

- the accounting obligations imposed on small and medium-sized firms;
- the accounting requirements of branches located in one member state if the company is established elsewhere, and
- the accounting requirements for partnerships and unlimited companies all of whose members with unlimited liability are limited companies.

### How?

The main way in which the finance function will be affected by EC company law policy is:

#### Accounting requirements

A Directive adopted in 1990 amends the fourth Directive on annual accounts to extend the derogations currently available to small and medium-sized companies and to raise the financial limits defining such companies, and allows all companies to publish a duplicate copy of their accounts in ECU.

The eleventh Directive deals with disclosures to be made in an EC member state by the branches of companies registered in another member state or non-EC country. It could benefit UK companies with branches elsewhere in the EC. In particular, a branch could no longer be required to prepare and publish its own accounts. However, the eleventh Directive will require the disclosure of certain information relating to both the company and the branch that is not currently required under UK law. Similar disclosure requirements in respect of credit and financial institutions are dealt with in the bank branches Directive.

Another Directive, also adopted in 1990, requires the disclosure of accounting information by partnerships and unlimited companies, all of whose members with unlimited liability are limited companies. In the UK this will be most easily met by the limited companies consolidating their interests in partnerships in the usual way. If this is not to be done, separate partnership accounts will need to be published. Limited companies will also be required to disclose in the notes to their accounts information on these types of partnerships in which they have an interest.

## Further information

Turn to the Company law topic at p. 265 in Volume 2 for more detailed coverage of these measures.

# 7.6 Company taxation

## Are you affected?

Your business is affected if:

- you have subsidiaries, branches or firms in another member state;
- transactions for goods or services are made between any of your subsidiaries;
- you operate in the UK only;
- you own at least 75 per cent of the capital of a company in another member state;
- you own at least 25 per cent of the capital of a company in another member state.

## Why?

- The mergers Directive which came into force on 1 January 1992 provides for deferral of tax on capital gains from certain types of cross-border reorganisation within the Community.
- The new arbitration procedures agreed within the Community will eliminate double taxation on transactions between group members should there be a dispute over tax adjustments between tax authorities in different member states.
- The proposed Directive on carry over of losses, if adopted, would allow businesses greater relief for annual losses.
- The proposed Directive on cross-border losses, if adopted, would allow UK parent companies to claim tax relief for any losses incurred by their branches and subsidiaries in other member states.
- The Directive on parents and subsidiaries, which came into force on 1 January 1992, eliminates the double taxation of dividends paid by a subsidiary in one member state to its parent in another, and abolishes withholding tax (tax deducted at source) on such dividends.

The Community is considering a proposed Directive to eliminate withholding taxes on cross-border interest and royalty payments.

## How?

### Eliminating tax differences in the Community

The Directive on the taxation of cross-border mergers and demergers, effective from 1 January 1992, allows you to defer liabilities on capital gains which could otherwise arise on certain types of company reorganisations you may undertake. The types of reorganisations covered are mergers, demergers, asset transfers and exchanges of shares between companies in different member states.

For such transactions it will often be possible for companies to defer liability on capital gains until the newly acquired asset is disposed of.

Tax authorities challenge the inter-company pricing policies of multinational companies when they suspect that the pricing of goods and services exchanged within the group has transferred profits from one country to another (transfer pricing).

If this leads to an adjustment by a tax authority in a company's taxable profit which is not matched by the tax authority in the other state, double taxation may occur. While there are some formal agreements for resolving such disputes, under the current procedure:

- tax authorities in the relevant member states are not required to reach agreement;
- there are no defined timescales for reaching agreement;
- the taxpayer is not involved in these negotiations.

The Arbitration Convention is designed to provide a procedure for resolving pricing disputes within the Community. It provides for discussions between the tax authorities concerned, and a mandatory arbitration procedure should agreement not be reached.

While relief for branch losses in other member states is already available under UK tax law, relief for losses of subsidiaries would allow subsidiaries' tax losses in another member state to be deducted from profits taxable by the UK. Profits made subsequently by those subsidiaries would be subject to tax in the UK to the limit of losses previously allowed.

All businesses may be allowed to set their annual net losses off against net profits of the previous three years. If, after this, any amount of losses remained unrelieved, businesses would be allowed relief against any profits in later years.

There is considerable uncertainty as to whether these proposals will be agreed.

Subsidiaries may, under the parent and subsidiary Directive, pay dividends free of withholding tax (tax deducted at source) to their parent company in any member state, although there are special rules for subsidiaries in Germany, Portugal and Greece. The parent will either not be taxed on these, or will have deducted from the tax payable a tax credit proportional to the tax paid on the subsidiary's profits which gave rise to the dividends.

If the proposed interest and royalties Directive were to be agreed, payments of interest and royalties between parent and subsidiary companies resident in different member states would be free of withholding tax (with exceptions for Greece and Portugal).

## Further information

Turn to the Company taxation topic at p. 287 in Volume 2 for more detailed coverage of these measures.

# 7.7 Financial services

## Are you affected?
Your business is affected if:
- you purchase banking products and services;
- you purchase investment services.

## Why?
- Community legislation covering financial services providers within the Community is likely to lead to a general increase in:
  - the number of firms offering 'pan-Community' financial products and services;
  - the range of financial products and services aimed at the corporate client;
  - the value and quality of services offered.
- Community legislation covering investment will increase your choice of products and banking and investment services on offer both within the UK and from other member states.

## How?
The main ways in which the purchasing function will be affected by EC financial services policy measures are:

### The opening up of the banking sector
The second banking co-ordination Directive allows credit institutions (broadly speaking, banks and building societies) and certain of their subsidiaries to establish a branch in, or provide a broad range of banking and financial services to any member state on the basis of their home EC state authorisation through the mechanism of the so-called 'single passport' – or banking licence.

For institutions to receive this passport, they must meet minimum standards of authorisation and supervision, laid down in the Directive.

While an increase in the number of credit institutions to which they have access will increase consumers' choice, it is likely that suppliers will generally compete on the quality of their services, rather than focusing on price.

### The opening up of the investment services sector
The investment services Directive will allow investment firms (as defined) to establish a branch in, or provide a range of investment services in, any member state on the basis of their home EC state authorisation – a similar 'single passport' to that for banks. For firms to be eligible for this passport

they must comply with certain minimum standards of authorisation and supervision, laid down in the Directive.

The Directive also includes minimum standards for Community banks' and investment firms' access to membership of Community stock exchanges and other regulated securities markets.

Although it is unlikely that the number of investment services providers will increase significantly as a result of this legislation, the nature of their offerings may change to reflect the increasing importance of Community trade to UK companies.

## Further information

Turn to the Financial services topic at p. 299 in Volume 2 for more detailed coverage of these measures.

# 7.8 Insurance

## Are you affected?

Your business is affected if:

- you purchase non-life insurance;
- you purchase motor insurance.
- you purchase life assurance.

## Why?

- The second non-life insurance Directive (implemented in July 1990 in the UK) introduced arrangements under which an insurance company could sell non-life insurance (other than motor insurance) to customers in another member state on a services basis, that is, without having an establishment in that state after having notified the supervisory authorities of that state. The third non-life insurance Directive, adopted in June 1992, introduces a single-licence system, enabling insurance companies whose head office is situated in a member state to carry on non-life insurance business throughout the Community, subject only to a single authorisation granted by their home state authorities and notification to the supervisory authorities of each member state in which it is to sell insurance.

- A series of three Directives, the first, second and third motor insurance Directives, achieve a high degree of harmonisation of members states' laws on compulsory motor insurance. The motor insurance services Directive, implemented in the UK in November 1992, extends the regime introduced by the second non-life insurance Directive to motor insurance.

- The second life insurance Directive introduces the same regime as the second non-life insurance Directive but for life assurance (with the exclusion of pension fund management) and is due to be implemented by 21 May 1993. A further Directive, adopted in November 1992 (the third life assurance Directive), introduces a single licence system for companies selling life assurance and enables such companies with head offices in member states to carry on life insurance business throughout the Community subject only to a single authorisation granted by their home state authorities and notification to the authorities of the member states in which the policies are to be sold.

These Directives should open up the Community market for insurance products and increase the pressure on insurers to offer high value and quality insurance products.

## How?

The main ways in which the purchasing function will be affected by insurance measures are:

### Increased choice of non-life insurance products

The second non-life insurance Directive provides a regulatory framework within which most non-life risks may be covered on a cross-frontier basis.

The third non-life insurance Directive will provide a single licence system for non-life insurance. Under the single licence, insurers with a head office in any member state will be able to provide direct non-life insurance throughout the Community on the strength of its home state authorisation.

Despite the potential increase in competition resulting from this opening up of the Community market, it is unlikely that premiums offered by new entrants will be significantly cheaper than those offered already by companies in the UK. On the other hand, companies needing to insure risks in several member states should find it easier to obtain competitively priced cover matched to their needs, and should be able to cover such risks within a single policy if they so wish.

### Increased choice of motor insurance products

The motor insurance services Directive enables an insurer in one member state to cover motor liability risks in any other member state without needing to have a branch or subsidiary there.

The first, second and third motor insurance Directives achieve a high degree of harmonisation of member states' laws on compulsory motor insurance, to protect the parties insured and road accident victims.

The UK motor insurance market is already highly price competitive, but companies whose employees travel in other member states should benefit, since policies automatically provide third-party cover throughout the Community.

### Increased choice of life assurance products

Both the second and third life assurance Directives are aimed at opening up the Community market for life assurance products. The third life assurance Directive extensively modifies the regimes created by previous Directives by introducing a single-licence system. An insurer with a head office in any member state will be able to provide life assurance anywhere in the Community either on a cross-frontier basis, or through local establishment on the strength of its home state authorisation.

Although this should increase choice for purchasers of life assurance, you may not see many cost benefits as the UK market is already among the most liberalised in the Community, and is highly price competitive.

## Further information

Turn to the Insurance topic at p. 319 in Volume 2 for more detailed coverage of this area.

# 7.9 Pharmaceuticals

## Are you affected?

Your business is affected if:

- you develop new medicinal products for human or veterinary use which are likely to be marketed in more than one member state;
- the effective patent life of your products has been reduced because of the delay occurred in obtaining market authorisation.

## Why?

- The Council of Ministers has reached agreement on a package of proposals, known as 'Future Systems', which, from around 1995, will begin to harmonise licensing decisions across the Community. There will be a centralised procedure for certain types of new medicines, such as those derived from biotechnology, whereby licensing decisions will be made by Community bodies and will be binding in all member states. For all other medicines (except homoeopathics), a decentralised procedure will operate, based on mutual recognition of national licensing decisions with binding arbitration by Community bodies where member states disagree over a decision. The new procedures will be supported by a European Medicines Evaluation Agency (EMEA).
- The Community has agreed to allow firms to apply for a 'supplementary protection certificate' which provides an extension to the effective patent life of a product. This will compensate, in part at least, for the patent life lost in obtaining market authorisation for a new product. This should benefit you in terms of returns on your investment.

## How?

The main ways in which the finance function will be affected by pharmaceuticals measures are:

### Product licences

The 'Future Systems' arrangements should help to reduce the costs involved in applying for marketing authorisations in more than one member state. For medicinal products subject to the centralised procedure, you will be able to apply for a single licence which will be valid throughout the Community. For other products, the decentralised procedure will provide a quicker and more effective way to apply for licences in more than one member state.

### Patent life

The 'supplementary protection certificate' will restore to your patented medicinal products some of the patent term which is lost while a marketing authorisation is being obtained. The certificate will give most products an effective patent life of 15 years from the date at which it first begins to sell on the market, subject to the extension not being more than five years.

## Further information

Turn to the Pharmaceuticals topic at p. 381 in Volume 2 for more detailed coverage of these measures and proposals.

# 7.10 Structural funds

## Are you affected?
Your business is affected if:
- any of your operations are located in an area which has traditionally produced coal or steel, in one of the least prosperous regions of the Community, or in a rural area;
- you are likely to invest in innovatory projects or projects which can be considered to further the development of the less-favoured regions, improve communications, improve the environment, improve the competitiveness of Community industry, or attain the Community's energy policy objectives;
- you are a small or medium-sized company.

## Why?
- The European Coal and Steel Community offers financial assistance to companies in the form of grants, loans and guarantees to improve economic and social conditions in the coal and steel producing regions. The European Regional Development Fund provides support, via the Department of Trade and Industry, for industrial investment in small firms in designated areas and via the Department of the Environment, and Welsh and Scottish offices for infrastructure projects, local initiatives, studies/technical assistance/pilot schemes, and environmental protection measures. Funding is also available via the Ministry for Agriculture, Fisheries and Food developments,
- The European Investment Bank offers cheap loans for small and medium-sized companies and other larger firms (for projects which further the development of the Community).

## How?
The structural funds, the European Investment Bank and the European Coal and Steel Community provide financial assistance for certain types of project or specific geographic areas. You should be aware of any help which you could be entitled to before making investment decisions.

## Further information
Turn to the Structural funds topic at p. 343 for more detailed coverage of these sources of funding.

# 8 · The **CORPORATE AFFAIRS** function

| | | |
|---|---|---|
| 8.1 | Free movement of goods, people, services and capital | 157 |
| 8.2 | Standards | 159 |
| 8.3 | Trade policy and customs duties | 161 |
| 8.4 | Employment | 162 |
| 8.5 | Public procurement | 163 |
| 8.6 | Environmental policy | 166 |
| 8.7 | Consumer protection | 167 |
| 8.8 | Intellectual property | 169 |
| 8.9 | Information technologies and telecommunications | 171 |
| 8.10 | Company law | 172 |
| 8.11 | Financial services | 175 |
| 8.12 | State aids | 177 |
| 8.13 | Structural funds | 178 |
| 8.14 | Competition policy | 179 |
| 8.15 | Pharmaceuticals | 182 |

# 8.1 Free movement of goods, people, services and capital

## Are you affected?

Your business is affected if:

- you consider that you are facing illegal barriers to trade in other member states.

## Why?

In order to eliminate obstacles to the free movement of goods, the Community has established the rule that, subject to certain conditions, member states should not maintain or erect barriers to trade.

This principle is set out in Arts. 30 and 34 of the Treaty of Rome and, over the years, a large body of European Court case law has dynamically interpreted these Articles. The provisions of Arts. 30 and 34 should make it easier for you to trade in other member states.

## How?

The main ways in which the corporate affairs function may be affected by the free movement of goods rules are:

### Illegal trade practices

Articles 30 and 34 of the Treaty of Rome established the principles that member states cannot introduce or maintain quantitative restrictions (or measures which have an equivalent effect) on imports from and exports to other member states. Many of the actions concerning breaches of these Articles have their origin in individual complaints by firms in member states.

If you are facing illegal trade practices in other member states, you should refer the case to the DTI's Single Market Compliance Unit (SMCU) or to the Commission. The SMCU will advise and assist in taking action with other member states' governments and with the Commission.

Trade barriers can also be challenged through the member states' national courts, and these courts can refer to the European Court of Justice for preliminary rulings on the compatibility of trade barriers with the Treaty Articles.

### Permissible trade restrictions

You should also be aware that some trade restrictions may be permissible. For example, Art. 36 of the Treaty of Rome allows member states to place prohibitions or restrictions on imports, exports or goods in transit on specified grounds such as the protection of human, animal or plant health, public morality, public security, industrial or intellectual property rights. However, these are only permitted if they do not represent arbitrary discrimination against products from other member states or a disguised restriction on trade.

## Further information

Turn to the Free movement of goods, people, services and capital topic at p. 1 in Volume 2 for more detailed coverage of these measures.

# 8.2 Standards

## Are you affected?

Your business is affected if:

- your products carry CE marking;
- your products conform to a national or European regulatory standard.

## Why?

- The Commission is proposing to reconcile the Directives adopted under the New Approach to remove inconsistencies between them in the provisions for CE marking. If adopted, you will have to comply with any changes made to CE marking rules.
- The Community is trying to prevent the establishment of new technical regulations which could constitute barriers to trade within the Community. Member states are required to notify the Commission in draft of any new technical regulations relating to any industrial or agricultural product. It is open to other member states to object if they consider that they constitute technical barriers to trade. The UK can only make its views known if UK industry ensures that it keeps abreast of current developments and communicates objections to the DTI.

## How?

The main ways in which the corporate affairs function will be affected by EC standards measures are:

### CE marking – proposed reconciliation of Directives

In the current proposal, your product must conform to essential requirements and must be CE marked. You must therefore arrange to have one put in place if you do not already carry one. You may also have to affix the identification number of the organisation which tested or certified your product. Finally, other marks which you may currently use may be affected by the proposal. You may therefore wish to monitor the outcome of the proposed Regulation to ensure your compliance.

### New standards as barriers to trade

New approach Directives outline the essential requirements that a product must meet in order to be sold in the Community. Under Community law, member state authorities are required to accept products which conform to the legislation and standards of other member states where these are intended to achieve equivalent objectives on their market. However, the same principle of 'mutual recognition' cannot be applied to the individual purchaser in the market who is free to set his own requirements, often by reference to national standards (not implementing European standards).

You can object to a developing 'industrial standard' on the basis that it will constitute a barrier to trade in any new national regulations of member states. There are a number of ways in which you can keep abreast of developments: the DTI circulates details of draft new technical regulations through various government departments to those most likely to be affected. Brief details are also published weekly by the Association of British Chambers of Commerce in 'Business Briefing'. They are also available on Spearhead, the DTI's single market database.

## Further information

Turn to the Standards topic at p. 13 in Volume 2 for more detailed coverage of this measure and proposal.

# 8.3 Trade policy and customs duties

## Are you affected?
Your business is affected if:
- you import goods from outside the Community;
- your products are in direct competition with goods imported from outside the Community.

## Why?
- Further changes are being made to the Community's customs procedures to take account of changes resulting from the completion of the single market and to harmonise these procedures.
- You may believe that you are losing market share to cheap imports from outside the Community.

## How?
The main ways in which the corporate affairs function will be affected by EC trade and customs duties policy are:

### Community customs code
A proposal to bring all the basic principles of existing Community customs legislation into a single body of law has been put forward. The intended result of this is to make the rules governing trade between the Community and other countries clearer. In addition, the proposal would also introduce a right of appeal against decisions taken by customs authorities. In the future, this should provide you with a form of redress if you feel that the customs authorities have made an unfair decision against you.

### Anti-dumping and countervailing duties
Anti-dumping and countervailing duties are designed to protect Community products from unfair competition. Anti-dumping duties are levied against goods which are imported into the Community below their domestic price. Countervailing duties are levied against goods which have been subsidised by the exporting country.

If you believe that your products are being unfairly discriminated against in this way, you should approach either the DTI or the Commission.

## Further information
Turn to the Trade and customs duties topic at p. 79 in Volume 2 for more detailed coverage of this measure and proposal.

# 8.4 Employment

## Are you affected?

Your business is affected if:

- you have operations in more than one member state and employ more than 1,000 employees.

## Why?

Companies or groups of companies in the Community which operate in more than one member state and are above a specified size would be required, at the request of the employees or their representatives, to inform and consult with their employees through European Works Councils. These would be bodies which act as representatives of the companies' employees and would have to be informed or consulted on any management proposal concerning the undertaking as a whole, or at affecting establishments in two members states and likely to have serious consequences for the interests of employees.

## How?

The main way in which the corporate affairs function will be affected by EC employment policy is:

### European Works Councils

The Commission proposes to establish in large companies and groups of companies European Works Councils as a mechanism for informing and consulting with employees. The proposal would apply to:

- companies with a minimum of 1,000 employees in the Community and 100 employees in at least each of two member states;
- groups of companies with a minimum of 1,000 employees within the Community and at least two group companies in different member states each of which employs at least 100 employees within the Community.

The proposal, if adopted, would introduce a new tier of employee representation at European level.

## Further information

Turn to the Employment topic at p. 105 in Volume 2 for more detailed coverage of this proposal.

# 8.5 Public procurement

## Are you affected?

Your business is affected if:

- you could sell to local or central government;
- you could sell to utilities, operate water, electricity, gas, telecommunications or transport networks providing services to the public;
- you are part of an organisation with a licence covering exploration or extraction of oil, gas or solid fuel;
- you are part of an organisation operating a port or airport (that is, providing terminal facilities to transport carriers by air, sea or inland waterways);
- you believe that one of these organisations has not followed the relevant procedures and that you have been unfairly treated.

## Why?

The strengthening of public procurement legislation is providing new forms of redress for suppliers who consider they have been harmed or are at risk of harm from a breach of the rules. For example, if a supplier thinks he has been excluded improperly, he can seek redress through the appropriate review body or the court. The Commission also has powers to take member states to the European Court of Justice for non-compliance with the public procurement rules.

The corporate affairs function may wish to make itself aware of the appropriate forms of redress in these circumstances.

## How?

The main ways in which the corporate affairs function will be affected by EC public procurement rules are:

### Your customers

If you have any of the following kinds of customers, they have to comply with the public procurement rules:

- central, regional and local government;
- other governmental bodies such as health services and police forces;
- any public organisation coming within the GATT agreement on government procurement (GPA);
- publicly and privately owned utilities.

In certain circumstances, purchasers are obliged to tell you, the seller, why your bid has failed.

### Products

The following products and services are covered by the public procurement rules:

- building and civil engineering works;
- supplies of goods on purchase or hire;
- a wide range of services such as consultancy and computer services, accounting, cleaning, property maintenance and refuse disposal, from 1 July 1993.

Contracts below the following thresholds will not be covered:

- *Supplies and services*:
  regional and local government: approx. £140,000;
  central government and other bodies covered by GPA: approx. £88,000;
- building works including works divided into lots: approx. £3.5m;
- *Utilities*:
  supplies to the telecommunications sector: approx. £420,000;
  supplies to other sectors: approx. £280,000;
  building works approx. £3.5m.

The following hierarchy of standards must be used in the public sector:

- national standards implementing European standards;
- national standards implementing international standards;
- national standards;
- any other standards.

The utilities must use:

- national standards;
- other recognised standards.

### Selling procedures

How you sell your products or services will be affected by the following procedures which organisations must use when purchasing:

- *Advertising rules*: in the public sector all tenders above the financial thresholds must be advertised in the *Official Journal of the European Communities*. This information is also available from Tenders Electronic Daily.
  In the utilities sector, purchasers may advertise qualification systems or invite interest through periodic indicative notices.
- *Tendering procedures*: purchasers may use open, restricted or (in the utilities sector and, in certain cases, in the public sector) negotiated procedures.
- *Qualifications*: suppliers may be asked to meet conditions laid down by the purchaser by giving evidence of business, financial or technical standing.

- *Award criteria*: the criteria are price alone, or a combination of factors which makes the tender the 'most economically advantageous'. These might include, for example, a combination of price, quality and delivery. Purchasers must say in advance what the criteria will be and abide by them when assessing bids.
- *Time limits*: the minimum time between first advertising a tender and the closing date is specified, and can vary between 37 and 52 days, depending on which procedure is used.
- *Compliance*: the compliance Directives ensure that firms who think they have been harmed by a breach of the rules will have the same level of legal protection in all member states. In the UK, redress will be through the courts.

## Further information

Turn to the Public procurement topic at p. 153 in Volume 2 for more detailed coverage of these measures.

# 8.6 Environmental policy

## Are you affected?

Your business is affected if:

- your organisation produces, imports, transports or otherwise handles waste products.

## Why?

A proposal from the Commission intends to impose civil liability for any damage caused by waste on the producer or, in certain circumstances the importer or transporter, irrespective of fault.

## How?

The main way in which the corporate affairs function will be affected by environmental policy is:

### Civil liability for damage caused by waste

A proposal from the Commission could affect the number of claims made against you for any damage to individuals, property or impairment of the environment caused by waste (but not by other forms of pollution, for example, air or water pollution). This would put pressure on you to set more stringent standards for the storage, transportation and disposal of waste. Your investors may also press for higher standards in your operation. Companies covered by the Directive will be required to be insured against the potential liability. It may also affect any existing insurance policy, since the potential number of claims made against you could increase. You should also take these risks into account before investing in, or taking over any company.

## Further information

Turn to the Environmental policy topic at p. 185 in Volume 2 for more detailed coverage of this proposal.

# 8.7 Consumer protection

## Are you affected?
Your business is affected if:
- you sell products or services in the Community.

## Why?
When you enter into a contract with a customer, in many circumstances, the legislation of the consumer's country of residence now applies to many contracts covering goods and services.

The Community's consumer protection legislation aims to:
- strengthen the rights of consumers (usually defined so as to exclude business purchasers);
- provide them with improved legal redress if they suffer as a result of faulty goods.

As a result, you could be liable to legal action and the associated financial penalties if you are held responsible for selling defective or unsafe goods.

If Community legislation on the supply of services is adopted in its current form, people who suffer personal injury or material damage as a result of the service they bought, will find it easier to obtain damages from the supplier of the service.

## How?
The main ways in which the corporate affairs function will be affected by consumer protection measures are:

### Consumer contracts
Save for certain provisions, the Rome Convention on the law applicable to contractual obligations has the force of law in the UK by virtue of the Contracts (Applicable Law) Act 1990.

In general, the Rome Convention provides that the contract shall be governed by the law chosen by the parties. In the event of the law applicable not being chosen, the contract shall be governed by the law of the country with which it is most closely connected.

In the case of certain consumer contracts, subject to certain provisions, a choice of law made by the parties shall not have the result of depriving the consumer of the protection afforded to him by the mandatory rules of the law of the country in which he has his habit and residence. The Convention does not apply to certain types of contracts, including certain insurance contracts. The provisions for consumer contracts do not apply to contracts of carriage or contracts for the supply of services where the services are to be supplied to the consumer exclusively in a country other than that in which he has his habitual residence. Spain and Portugal are not signatories to the Rome Convention.

### Increased legal rights for customers

There are two key pieces of Community legislation which aim to improve consumer protection against defective or unsafe products. These are:

- the product liability Directive, which was implemented in the UK by Part I, Consumer Protection Act 1987. This introduced strict liability for the manufacturers of products which cause personal injury or material damage. Strict liability means that the injured party need not prove the producer's negligence or fault;
- the general product safety Directive, which complements the product liability Directive. This increases consumer protection by requiring Community countries to introduce a general obligation on manufacturers, importers and, in certain circumstances, others in the supply chain, to supply only safe consumer products. This Directive was adopted on 29 June 1992 and must be implemented by 29 June 1997.

In light of these developments, firms are increasingly beginning to:

- minimise their product liability exposure by the use of design review systems and regular audits of company product safety systems;
- review and respond to customer complaints promptly, as this also helps to identify potential problems with products.

Parent companies with subsidiaries trading in the Community may need to think about methods of protecting themselves from claims made against the subsidiaries.

### Improved legal position for service buyers

The proposed Directive on the liability of suppliers of services seeks to impose liability for damage caused by fault committed in performance of a service. It would require a supplier of services to prove that he was not at fault should the supply of a service result in injury or damage to the person receiving the service or to his personal property. The injured party would only have to prove that damage had occurred and that it resulted from the provision of a service. The proposal would require suppliers of services to ensure that services are performed to standards of safety which consumers can reasonably expect.

The proposed Directive would cover all services provided on a professional basis or by way of a public service and in an independent manner, whether or not in return for payment. There are a number of exclusions including public services designed to maintain public security and sectors already covered by Directives, such as package travel and treatment of waste.

## Further information

Turn to the Consumer protection topic at p. 203 in Volume 2 for more detailed coverage of these measures and proposals.

# 8.8 Intellectual property

## Are you affected?

Your business is affected if:

- you consider that your trade mark or patent rights are being infringed in a member state;
- you manufacture, supply or use computer programs, that is, software.

## Why?

- The Community Patent Convention, under which Community patents would be granted, will designate Community patent courts in all member states. When it enters into force, any litigation after grant will take place under the Convention rather than under national laws.

    The Commission has also proposed the creation of a Community trade mark, which would enable businesses to secure Community-wide protection for their trade marks through a single application to a Community Trade Mark Office. Community trade mark courts would be designated in all member states and their judgments would be valid throughout the Community.

- The Community has sought to harmonise software copyright laws in the member states to ensure a common standard of protection for computer programs. The software Directive (which is implemented by the Copyright (Computer Programs) Regulations 1992) provides for decompilation without authorisation of the copyright owner to reproduce and translate a program code in order to obtain information on interfaces so as to create new programs which are compatible and interoperable with existing systems. Provision is also made for the correction of program errors and making back-up copies.

## How?

The main ways in which the corporate affairs function will be affected by EC intellectual property policy are:

### Community patents

If you consider that another business is infringing your patent rights in another member state, the ratification of the Community Patent Convention will enable you to obtain a judgment from one of the Community patent courts established in each member state. The judgments of these courts will have effect throughout the Community.

### Community trade marks

If you consider that another business is infringing your Community trade mark, you will be able to obtain a judgment from one of the Community trade mark courts established in each member state. The judgments of these Courts will have effect throughout the Community.

### The software Directive

Decompilation without authorisation of the copyright owner is limited strictly to achieving interoperability and the Directive makes it clear that anybody exercising this right must take great care not to copy the expression of a program or otherwise infringe copyright. The use of this form of reverse engineering is only permitted where it is indispensable for obtaining the necessary information for interoperability, and given that the information is not previously readily available.

You may wish to seek expert advice on your decompilation rights and on reverse engineering to ensure that you comply with the Directive, and to avoid litigation.

## Further information

Turn to the Intellectual property topic at p. 225 in Volume 2 for more detailed coverage of these measures.

# 8.9 Information technologies and telecommunications

## Are you affected?

Your business is affected if:

- any part of your company uses personal information held on computer or other manual filing system in the course of its work.

## Why?

The series of proposals from the Commission regarding personal data protection are intended to make sure that personal data held on computer does not infringe privacy rights. If these proposals become law, databases of customer information used in any part of your company will be affected. You will, therefore, have to comply with these proposals if they become law, and you may be restricted in the ways that you use the information that you hold.

## How?

The main way in which the corporate affairs function will be affected by EC information technologies and telecommunications policy is:

### Customer information

Current proposals on data protection would restrict your use of market information, including the use of direct mailing techniques, approaching potential customers on the basis of information from other sources, transfer of data to non-Community countries, and, possibly, the extent and type of access to information from other parts of the organisation. This will have legal compliance implications for you if they are adopted. The UK government's position on these proposals is that those parts of it which go beyond the Convention on Data Protection (and, therefore, the Data Protection Act 1984) are unnecessary. Agreement on the Commission's proposals may take a considerable time.

## Further information

Turn to the Information technologies and telecommunications topic at p. 239 in Volume 2 for more detailed coverage of this proposal.

# 8.10 Company law

## Are you affected?

Your business is affected if:

- you operate outside the UK through branches in one or more member states;
- you have links with companies or firms in other member states which you wish to develop;
- you operate through a partnership in the UK or in another member state;
- you are a partnership and all your members with unlimited liability are limited companies;
- you are a public limited company employing more than 1,000 employees;
- you are an individual entrepreneur interested in limiting your liability.

## Why?

- If you carry out business outside the UK through a branch, or if you intend to set up a branch elsewhere in the EC, you will be affected by the implementation of the eleventh Directive and the bank branches Directive which seeks to harmonise registration and accounting obligations imposed on the branches of companies and credit and financial institutions registered in another member state or non-EC country. The Directives limit the requirements which member states can impose on the branches of foreign companies.
- You may also want to investigate creating a European Economic Interest Grouping (EEIG). The EEIG allows the creation of a new type of business association between two or more businesses primarily functioning in two or more member states.
- The Community is discussing the European Company Statute (ECS) which, if adopted, would give companies in different member states the option of forming a European company under a framework of Community and national law.
- If you carry on business through a partnership or an unlimited company or if you are a partnership you will be affected by the implementation of the partnerships Directive which seeks to harmonise the accounting obligations placed on partnerships made up entirely of limited companies and on limited companies involved in such partnerships.
- The proposal for a fifth Directive would, if adopted, affect all public limited companies. The proposal covers the management and structure of PLCs and would affect the decision-making process in your business. As drafted at present, it would require compulsory worker

participation (according to one of a limited number of specified models). The worker participation models would apply, at the request of employees, in companies employing more than 1,000 employees.
- If you are an individual entrepreneur wishing to limit your liability, you may benefit from the implementation of the twelfth Directive which requires member states to allow the formation of single-member private limited companies.

## How?

The main ways in which the corporate affairs function will be affected by EC company law are:

### Cross-border activities

The European Economic Interest Grouping (EEIG) may help you build links and to co-operate with companies, firms or individuals in other member states over a broad range of activities without merging or forming a joint subsidiary.

If your company is established in more than one member state, or wishes to set up or take part in operations with companies in other member states, the proposed European Company Statute would, if adopted, allow you to form a European company which might assist you in these aims.

### Cross-border activity through a branch

The eleventh Directive and the bank branches Directive will limit the financial and business reporting requirements that can be imposed on the branches of UK companies and credit and financial institutes.

The Eleventh Directive prevents the imposition of onerous reporting or accounting requirements on the branches of foreign companies. This may help your company if you have branches established in other member states. In particular, your branch(es) would no longer be required to prepare and publish separate accounts relating to its operations and the accounts to be filed are those prepared by your company for filing in the UK.

### Structure and management of public limited companies

If you are a public limited company, the proposal for a fifth Directive could affect your business decision-making process by requiring you to choose between board structures which are substantially different from the UK unitary board. Agreement on the Directive does not appear likely to be reached soon.

The fifth Directive would, at the request of the employees, also require compulsory employee representation in decision making.

### Single-member private limited companies

If you are an individual entrepreneur interested in limiting your liability, you may benefit from the implementation of the twelfth Directive which allows private limited companies to have a single member.

Before implementation, UK law required at least two persons to set up such a company.

### Activities through a partnership

The partnerships Directive requires the publication of accounting information about partnerships or unlimited companies whose members with unlimited liability are all limited companies. If you are involved in such an organisation in the UK you may either consolidate your interest in it in your accounts, publish its accounts with your own accounts, or arrange for their separate publication. You will have to disclose in your own accounts the fact of your involvement in any such partnerships. You will be able to find out information on these types of partnerships in other member states once the Directive has been implemented by 1995.

## Further information

Turn to the Company law topic at p. 265 in Volume 2 for more detailed coverage of these measures and proposals.

# 8.11 Financial services

## Are you affected?
Your business is affected if:
- you have a major shareholding in a company listed and incorporated in the Community;
- shares in your company are quoted on the stock exchange;
- you are considering offering transferable securities to the public.

## Why?
- A Directive requires those with major holdings in companies listed and incorporated in the Community to inform the companies when their holding exceeds, or falls below, certain thresholds.
- A Directive on prospectuses specifies the information to be published when transferable securities are offered to the public for the first time, co-ordinating requirements in member states for the drawing up, scrutiny and distribution of these prospectuses. It also provides for this mutual recognition of certain prospectuses within the EC.
- Recent Community legislation also provides for the recognition of certain public-offer prospectuses as stock exchange listing particulars in any member state.

## How?
The main ways in which the corporate affairs function will be affected by EC financial services measures are:

### The disclosure of shareholdings
The Directive on the disclosure of major shareholdings will require those with holdings in officially listed EC companies to disclose their holdings to the company when they exceed, or fall below, certain thresholds. This information must be disclosed to the public.

Certain changes need to be made to existing UK law on disclosure of interests in shares, in order to implement the Directive.

### The preparation of prospectuses
The prospectus Directive requires a prospectus to be published when transferable securities are offered to the public for the first time in any member state, as long as the securities to be offered are not already listed on a stock exchange in that member state. It specifies the information to be included and provides for the mutual recognition of certain prospectuses within the EC. It also allows for the Community to enter into agreements with countries outside the Community for recognition of each other's prospectuses.

The listing particulars Directive co-ordinates specific requirements for the drawing up, scrutiny and distribution of particulars for official listing on a stock exchange in the Community. Subsequent amendments provide for the mutual recognition of such particulars approved in one member state, and for the mutual recognition of public-offer prospectuses as listing particulars.

## Further information

Turn to the Financial services topic at p. 299 in Volume 2 for more detailed coverage of these measures.

# 8.12 State aids

## Are you affected?
Your business is affected if:
- you operate in a sector where the Commission applies special restrictions on the kind and level of Government support available to you and other EEA competitors.

## Why?
The Commission has considerable powers to monitor and limit all forms of aid and support from member states that potentially distort competition in the Community. There are a number of specially earmarked sectors and types of aid (for example, the automotive and synthetic fibres sectors, and aid for environmental protection and for research and development) where important restrictions and conditions have been applied. These are being continuously developed, by new or revised rules and legal precedents. These set an evolving legal and industrial framework for what all member states can and cannot do in support of their industries which you will want to be aware of as an increasingly important part of the ground rules for competition in the single market.

## How?
The main ways in which the corporate affairs function will be affected by EC state aid policy are:

### Government support
The Commission's approach to different kinds of aid and any special rules relating to your sector set important constraints on the support that can be given by the UK government, as well as by all other member states.

### Competitors
If, through your sales and marketing activities, you identify unfairly subsidised competitors, you should consider making a complaint to the Commission. Your trade association and the DTI can advise you on this.

### Opportunities to influence future rules
The Commission's commitment to keeping the state aid rules under constant review creates openings for you and others in your industry to press for tighter control on particular forms of aid that might disadvantage you unfairly in competition with other countries in the Community.

## Further information
Turn to the State aids topic at p. 333 in Volume 2 for more detailed coverage of these measures.

# 8.13 Structural funds

### Are you affected?

Your business is affected if:

- any of your operations are located in an area which has traditionally produced coal or steel, in one of the least prosperous regions of the Community, or in a rural area;
- you are likely to invest in innovatory projects or projects which can be considered to further the development of the less-favoured regions or improve communications, the environment or the competitiveness of Community industry, or attain the Community's energy policy aims;
- you are a small or medium-sized enterprise.

### Why?

- The European Coal and Steel Community offers financial assistance to companies in the form of grants, loans and guarantees to improve economic and social conditions in coal and steel producing regions. The European Regional Development Fund provides support, through the DTI, for industrial investment in small firms in designated areas, and via the Department of the Environment, and the Scottish and Welsh Offices for infrastructure projects, local initiatives, studies/technical assistance/pilot schemes, and environmental protection measures. Funding is also available for agricultural and fishery developments from the Ministry for Agriculture, Fisheries and Food.
- The European Investment Bank offers cheap loans for small and medium-sized enterprises and other larger firms (for projects which further the development of the Community).

### How?

Structural funds, the European Investment Bank and the European Coal and Steel Community provide financial assistance for certain types of project or specific geographic areas. You should be aware of any help which you could be entitled to before making investment decisions.

### Further information

Turn to the Structural funds topic at p. 343 in Volume 2 for more detailed coverage of these funds.

# 8.14 Competition policy

## Are you affected?

Your business is affected if:

- one of your products holds more than a 10 per cent share of the market in any substantial part of the Community;
- you are considering merging with another company in the Community;
- you have agreements with another company in the Community;
- you are considering entering into a joint venture with another company in the Community.

## Why?

- Article 86 of the Treaty of Rome prohibits firms from abusing a dominant market position which may affect trade between member states. Holding a dominant position does not, in itself, break EC competition rules: it is the abuse of such a position which breaks the rules and the Commission has powers to impose severe penalties on firms for such abuse.

  Dominance means, broadly, the power to behave independently in the relevant market. It is likely that firms holding more than 40 per cent of a particular market would be considered as having a dominant market share. The figure could, however, be much lower. Guidance is available from previous European Court and Commission decisions.

- If you are considering merging with another company, you should be aware that the Community has introduced a merger control regime which gives the Commission powers to vet mergers which are large enough to have a 'Community dimension', that is, where the turnovers of the firms involved exceed certain financial thresholds.

- Article 85 of the Treaty of Rome prohibits agreements between firms which may distort or restrict competition within the Community if trade between member states may be affected. Certain categories of agreements are, however, exempt from the prohibition in Art. 85. These are covered by Regulations known as block exemptions and include certain types of franchising and licensing agreements. Specific individual exemptions may also be granted on application to the European Commission.

- By definition, joint ventures require an agreement between two or more firms, and so may be subject to Community competition policy. Joint ventures are subject to different competition rules, depending on the nature of the particular joint venture in question.

## How?

The main ways in which the corporate affairs function will be affected by EC competition policy are:

### Dominant market position

As the Commission is enforcing competition rules increasingly rigorously, it is important to ensure that your current business practices cannot be interpreted as 'abuses' of a dominant position and thus an infringement of Art. 86. If one of your products has more than a 40 per cent market share, you may hold a dominant position in that market, and your operations may come within the scope of Art. 86.

If you hold between 10 per cent and 40 per cent of your market, you could still be perceived as having a dominant position when other factors are taken into account, and your operations may also come within the scope of Art. 86.

### Merger control

If you are considering merging with another firm in the Community, you should be aware that your merger may be subject to Community law if it is large enough to be considered as having a Community dimension, that is, if it satisfies certain criteria in terms of turnover of the firms involved. If the merger creates or strengthens a dominant position as a result of which competition would be significantly impeded, it will be prevented by the Commission. Alternatively, the Commission may impose conditions to ensure that the merger is compatible with the common market. Mergers with a Community dimension must be notified to the Commission in advance.

Failure to notify within certain time limits may incur a fine.

### Agreements

When drafting an agreement with another company in the Community, it is advisable to try to bring it within the terms of one of the block exemptions, which give automatic exemption from the prohibition in Art. 85, so that the agreement need not be notified to the Commission. You should ensure that any current or intended agreement does not infringe Art. 85. If your agreement does not fall within a block exemption, but you consider it meets the conditions for an exemption, you must notify it to the Commission.

If you are a small organisation, many of the agreements you conclude with similar sized companies will not be considered as infringing Art. 85.

If you believe that agreements between other companies are restricting your own ability to compete effectively, you may bring this matter to the attention of the Commission. The Office of Fair Trading is able to advise on procedural and presentational points.

### Joint ventures

If your joint venture is 'concentrative', that is, it leads to a lasting change in the structure of the companies involved, it will be covered by the merger control Regulation, and you will be required to notify the Commission provided certain criteria in terms of turnover of the firms involved are met.

If your joint venture is 'co-operative', that is, where the competitive behaviour of the firms involved are co-ordinated, it is subject to Arts. 85 and 86 of the Treaty. The Commission is producing a notice setting out how these agreements will be handled.

Because of the ambiguous status of joint ventures under Community competition policy, discussion with the Commission is advisable. You may want to seek legal advice on this matter.

## Further information

Turn to the Competition policy topic at p. 351 in Volume 2 for more detailed coverage of these measures and proposals.

# 8.15 Pharmaceuticals

## Are you affected?

Your business is affected if:

- you market medicinal products for human or veterinary use.

## Why?

In order to improve the information available to consumers, the Community has adopted a number of rules regarding the labelling of medicinal products and the information published on package leaflets.

## How?

The main way in which the corporate affairs function will be affected by pharmaceuticals measures is:

### Customer information

If you market medicinal products in the EC, you must comply with the requirements of the Directives on the labelling of such products and the provision of a package leaflet. These requirements have important implications for product liability.

You should check with the Medicines Control Agency (or Veterinary Medicines Directorate) that the information you provide to patients (or veterinary surgeons) complies with Community measures.

## Further information

Turn to the Pharmaceuticals topic at p. 381 in Volume 2 for more detailed coverage of this measure.

# APPENDIXES

# I · The KNOW-HOW APPENDIX

## 1.1 How the EC works

### The member states

The European Community is a group of 12 countries bound together by three major international treaties and a number of smaller ones, the most important of which is the Treaty of Rome.

The Treaty of Rome was signed in 1957 by Belgium, France, Italy, Luxembourg, Netherlands and Germany. They were joined in 1973 by Denmark, Ireland and the United Kingdom, in 1981 by Greece and in 1986 by Portugal and Spain.

### The institutions

There are four main Community institutions: the Commission, the Council, the Parliament and the Court of Justice.

#### The Commission

The Commission:

- proposes Community policy and legislation;
- executes the decisions taken by the Council of Ministers and supervises the day-to-day running of Community policies;
- acts as the 'guardian of the Treaties' and can initiate action against member states which do not comply with EC rules;
- has its own powers under the Treaties in some areas, notably competition policy and the control of Government subsidies.

There are 17 members of the Commission, or Commissioners, headed by a President. They are all appointed by national governments, two from each of the larger member states and one from each of the others. They are not, however, national delegates, but must act in the interests of the Community as a whole.

Each Commissioner is in charge of an area of Community policy. Commissioners formulate proposals within their area of responsibility aimed at implementing the Treaties.

The Commission services are responsible for the technical preparation of legislation and its implementation. They are currently divided into 23 Directorates-General (DGs) and a number of specialised services. Each DG or service has one or more Commissioners responsible for its work.

Currently the DGs are as listed below, but changes are expected by 1 April 1993:

- *DG I*: external relations;
- *DG II*: economic and financial affairs;
- *DG III*: internal market and industrial affairs;
- *DG IV*: competition;
- *DG V*: employment, industrial relations and social affairs;
- *DG VI*: agriculture;

- *DG VII*: transport;
- *DG VIII*: development;
- *DG IX*: personnel and administration;
- *DG X*: audiovisual, information, communication and culture;
- *DG XI*: environment, nuclear safety and civil protection;
- *DG XII*: science, research and development;
- *DG XIII*: telecommunications, information industries and innovation;
- *DG XIV*: fisheries;
- *DG XV*: financial institutions and company law;
- *DG XVI*: regional policy;
- *DG XVII*: energy;
- *DG XVIII*: credit and investments;
- *DG XIX*: budgets;
- *DG XX*: financial control;
- *DG XXI*: customs union and indirect taxation;
- *DG XXII*: co-ordination of structural policies;
- *DG XXIII*: enterprise policy, distributive trades, tourism and co-operatives.

**The Council of Ministers**

The Council is the Community's principal decision-making body. In most cases it adopts legislation on the basis of propsals from the Commission.

Council meetings take place at several levels:

- *Councils or summits*: these take place at least twice a year and are attended by heads of state or government, foreign ministers and representatives from the Commission who meet to discuss broad areas of policy;
- *specialist councils*: these deal with particular areas of policy. They are attended by the relevant ministers from member states and by the Commission. Policy initiatives are discussed and legislation is formally adopted at these meetings;
- *COREPER I and COREPER II (Committee of Permanent Representatives)*: these meet weekly and consist of permanent representatives or deputy permanent representatives of each member state. They pave the way for political decisions to be taken by ministers;
- *Council working groups*: these are attended by officials from member states and from the permanent representations in Brussels. These groups are convened as necessary and there are usually about 150 working groups in operation during any given Presidency. They examine the issues in detail.

Council meetings are chaired by the member state holding the Presidency of the Community. Each member state holds this office in turn for a six-month period. Denmark holds the Presidency to 30 June 1993, followed by Belgium to 31 December 1993.

### The Parliament
The European Parliament is a directly elected body of 518 members, 81 of whom come from the UK. Its formal opinion is required on most proposals before they can be adopted by the Council. Most of the detailed work in Parliament is done by its specialist Committees which examine and draw up reports on Commission proposals before they are put to the Parliament as a whole.

### The European Court of Justice
The European Court of Justice (ECJ) rules on the interpretation and application of Community laws. It has 13 judges, including one from each Community country. A Court of First Instance has been established to relieve the ECJ of some of its excessive workload.

### Other bodies
There are three other main bodies:

- the *Economic and Social Committee*: an advisory body representing employers, trade unions and other interest groups (such as consumers) which has to be formally consulted by the Commission on proposals relating to economic and social matters;
- the *Court of Auditors* which examines and assesses the Community's revenue and expenditure;
- the *European Investment Bank*: the European Community's bank which lends money to finance capital investment projects.

## Types of legislation

Under the Treaties, the Council and the Commission may make Regulations, issue Directives, take Decisions, make Recommendations or deliver opinions.

- *Regulations* have general application and are directly applicable in all member states. They do not have to be confirmed by national parliaments in order to have binding legal effects. If there is a conflict between a Regulation and existing (or future) national law, the Regulation prevails.
- *Directives* are binding on member states as to the result to be achieved within a stated period, but leave the method of implementation to national governments. In itself, a Directive does not have legal force within member states, but may take direct effect if the Directive is not duly implemented.
- *Decisions* are specific to particular parties and are binding in their entirety on those to whom they are addressed, whether member states, companies or individuals. Decisions imposing financial obligations are enforceable in national courts.

- *Recommendations and opinions* have no binding force but merely state the view of the institution that issues them.

## The legislative process

Community legislation is the result of a complex and often lengthy process of consultation and negotiation. Before legislation is formally proposed, the Commission will often discuss its ideas informally with national experts, professional and business organisations and interested parties.

The formal process usually starts with proposals made by the Commission. The Council can, however, request the Commission to undertake studies or submit appropriate proposals. The proposals are then submitted to the Council which must usually consult the Parliament and the Economic and Social Committee.

Most single market proposals are subject to the co-operation procedure under which the Parliament gives two readings, once when the Commission proposal is submitted to the Council and again after the Council has reached an agreement in principle (a common position). The Parliament can propose amendments at both stages.

The Council can formally adopt the Commission proposal as drafted, request the Commission to amend it, amend it itself, reject it or simply take no decision.

There are three methods of decision-taking in Council depending on the nature of the proposal and the Treaty Article on which it is based. These are: unanimity, simple majority voting (at least seven member states in favour) and qualified majority (weighted voting based on the relative size of the member states by population). Most single market measures are subject to qualified majority voting.

*To find out how to have influence in the legislative process, see below.*

## Enforcing EC rules

The Commission has its own powers of enforcement in some areas, notably competition policy and state aid. In other areas such as illegal trade barriers (see p. 192), the Commission can initiate action against a member state which does not comply with EC rules.

### Competition policy

EC competition policy is designed to ensure that trade between member states takes place on the basis of free and fair competition, and that barriers to trade between member states, when dismantled, are not replaced by private barriers which fragment the single market.

Articles 85 and 86 of the Treaty of Rome lay down the essential requirements applicable to businesses. The rules are directly enforceable in the national courts of member states.

### State aid

The Treaty establishes the fundamental principle that aid granted by the governments of member states, in whatever form, is incompatible with the concept of a common market if it distorts competition in trade within the Community. Articles 92–94 of the Treaty lay down the mechanism for regulating such aid.

## 1.2 How business can play its part

### Influencing the legislative process

There are numerous opportunities during the legislative process to make representations and contributions to the discussions and negotiations on any proposal or policy initiative.

This might be done at any, or all, of the various stages of the legislative process: through a national trade association, chamber of commerce or interest group, through the appropriate European trade association, through the CBI or its European grouping UNICE, through an MP or a House of Commons Committee Member, via the relevant UK government department official and/or the desk officer in the UK Permanent Representation in Brussels, via the Commission services official primarily responsible, through the Commissioner and his/her staff, and via the appropriate members of the European Parliament.

For further advice and information refer to the DTI publication *Brussels can you hear me? Influencing decisions in the European Community*. The booklet develops five key points for success in Brussels:

- get in early;
- work with others;
- think European;
- be prepared;
- get involved.

It also describes the three key stages of:

- gathering information;
- drawing up an action plan; and
- making the necessary contacts.

(See p. 207 for more information.)

### Implementation of EC legislation

Once a Directive has been adopted, member states must implement the Directive into national legislation within a set period of time (usually two years). This Manual covers implementation and enforcement of EC legislation in the UK. Information on single market legislation is also available from Spearhead, the DTI's on-line database. A booklet giving details of Spearhead and how to access it is available from the DTI (see p. 207).

Companies may also need to find out how EC legislation is being implemented or enforced in other member states. This information is collected by the Commission and held on the CELEX database, which is the major authoritative database covering European Community law. CELEX can be accessed via a number of hosts but, unless you are a regular user of such databases, the easiest way to access this information will be by contacting your local EuroInfoCentre (see p. 198).

Information held on CELEX includes the title and date of national legislation to implement Directives. Copies of the legislation itself can be obtained by writing to the appropriate publishers of national legislation (see p. 206).

Companies should take legal advice before acting on information about implementation, and this may involve consulting a reputable firm of local lawyers. Your usual solicitor for business matters should be able to suggest suitable law firms in other member states, but if they cannot, you should contact the Law Society's Information Office (see p. 209). The Law Society of England and Wales will consult its list of 950 firms of solicitors who can advise business on single market issues. The Law Society of Northern Ireland and the Law Society of Scotland can provide similar help.

## Illegal trade barriers

One of the fundamental principles enshrined in the Treaty of Rome is that goods should be able to move freely throughout the Community and that there should be a free and competitive market for services. Member states must not maintain or erect barriers to trade or to the provision of services. Prohibited practices include discrimination between home-produced and foreign goods, discriminatory technical standards, testing procedures, or labelling requirements, discriminatory taxation regimes on goods. Discriminatory pricing or profit margin controls, requirements for import licences or similar procedures are also prohibited. However, agreeing EC legislation to eliminate barriers to trade will not achieve a genuine single market unless the rules are evenly and effectively enforced.

In order to ensure that EC policy is put into practice, the Commission monitors the transposition of EC law into national legislation, where this is necessary, to ensure that member states implement all EC legislation correctly and on time. It is for each member state to enforce EC legislation. The Commission tries to ensure fair play for all. Since 1986 it has issued over 4,000 letters of formal notice to governments about suspected breaches of EC rules. It also pursues individual complaints. The European Court of Justice (ECJ) in turn interprets and applies Community law.

# BUSINESS OPPORTUNITIES OFFERED BY THE SINGLE MARKET · 193

## Complaints of non-compliance

If a company, individual or organisation has reason to believe that another member state is failing to implement or consistently enforce any EC legislation, contact should be made with the Single Market Compliance Unit (SMCU) (see p. 000 for the address of the SMCU). If there appears to be a legal basis for complaint, and there is evidence to support it, the SMCU will review the case and advise on the best way to resolve the problem. The UK Government will usually take up the case bilaterally with the offending member state. However, if bilateral pressure does not resolve the problem, the SMCU will help the company prepare its complaint to the Commission. Individuals or companies are also free to approach the Commission with complaints at any time, or to seek recourse through the national courts.

If the Commission, after carrying out its own investigation, finds evidence of a breach of EC law, it may initiate infraction proceedings against the offending member state under Art. 169 of the Treaty of Rome. If the member state does not comply with the Commission's opinion, the matter may be brought before the European Court of Justice. The full process from Commission opinion to judgment can take two or three years, so where possible a bilateral resolution is more desirable.

## 1.3 How business can make the most of the opportunities offered by the single market

### Improved opportunities for trade

Over half of all the UK's overseas trade is with Western Europe. This trade is increasing, and there remains considerable room for growth in every EC market.

There are many sources of advice and information to help companies make the most of the opportunities that result from the development of the single market.

General information about selling to other member states is contained in the DTI's booklet *Trading within Europe*. It contains useful advice from beginning the groundwork to delivery, paperwork and getting paid. It also points to other sources of help such as the Overseas Trade Services in the DTI (see p. 207).

Regional offices of the DTI are a useful first step for those seeking advice or information about selling in Europe. See p. 195 for a list of these offices.

Information about trading rules and conditions in a particular member state can be provided by the appropriate country desk in Europe Division of the DTI. See p. 197 for details.

International Chambers of Commerce can provide an invaluable source of local knowledge for firms trading with another member state. This might include information and advice on market statistics, marketing, exporting or finding an agent. See p. 204 for a list of these.

## Public procurement contracts

Selling to public purchasers in the Community is big business: it comprises about 15 per cent of the gross domestic product of the EC (£506 billion at 1990 prices). EC heads of government recognised the importance of opening up public procurement and seven Directives have been proposed, six of which are in place or have been agreed in principle. When all the Directives are in force, the vast majority of public procurement contracts will be covered by the rules. These Directives also provide for procedures for recourse which offer speedy intervention if the rules are being breached.

The DTI has produced a booklet *A guide to public purchasing* to help companies take advantage of opportunities of public procurement contracts. The booklet answers four questions:

- where is the business?
- how do I go about getting the businesss?
- what are the rules governing purchasers? and
- what do I do if the rules are broken?

See p. 207.

There are several sources of contract notices, although only the *Official Journal* (OJ) is mandatory (they appear in the 'S' Series of the OJ). This daily publication carries about 400 or 500 contract notices every week. Copies of the OJ can be bought either singly or by subscription from HMSO (see p. 209).

Every contract notice published in the OJ can also be found on Tenders Electronic Daily (TED) which is an online data service provided by the Commission. Access is gained through the ECHO service which is available by subscription or via EuroInfoCentres (see p. 198).

All contract notices in the OJ are also fed into the database run by the Export Intelligence Service. Details can be obtained from DTI regional offices (see p. 195).

Other contract opportunities might arise in connection with the structural funds. They are intended to support investment in infrastructure, industry and agriculture in the least developed regions of the Community. The funds offer important opportunities to UK firms to develop their business in these markets. For further information contact DTI World Aid Section at Ashdown House, 123 Victoria Street, London SW1E 6RB or telephone 071 215 6157/6765.

## Further sources of information and documentation

- *European Information Centres* (EuroInfoCentres or EICs) have been set up by the Commission throughout the Community. There are over 200 in total in the 12 member states, 23 of which are in the UK, plus satellite offices. They act as links to supply companies with information on all aspects of Community affairs, its policies, regulations and prospects. The aim is to provide up-to-date information which is of direct relevance to business (see p. 198 for a list of EuroInfoCentres).

- The *European Commission* has four information offices in the UK which can signpost businesses to sources of European information. A full collection of EC papers and legislation can be inspected in office libraries (see p. 205).
- The *European Parliament*'s London Information Office can provide general information on the proceedings of the Parliament. The office's library has records of all debates in the original languages and Parliamentary reports. Addresses and telephone numbers of MEPs and details of their Committees are available from the office as well as from Citizen's Advice Bureaux, public libraries and local authority offices (see p. 206 for the address of the London Information Office).
- *European Documentation Centres* (EDCs), which are mainly to be found in university libraries, have substantial collections of the publicly available documentation of the European Communities. A full list of EDCs is available from the European Commission information office in London (see p. 205 for this address).

Sales and subscriptions of EC publications, such as the Official Journal, are made in the UK through HMSO. Details of directories and other useful publications are listed at p. 207).

## 1.4 Useful addresses

### DTI regional offices and country desks

Consulting these organisations is a useful first step for those seeking advice or information about selling in Europe.

**Regional offices**

- **DTI South East**
  Bridge Place
  88–89 Eccleston Square
  London
  SW1V 1PT

  Tel: 071 215 0574
  Fax: 071 215 0875

  Covers all Greater London boroughs.

- **DTI South East (Reading)**
  40 Caversham Road
  Reading
  Berkshire
  RG1 7EB

  Tel: 0734 395600
  Fax: 0734 502818

  Covers Hampshire, Berkshire, Buckinghamshire, Oxfordshire and Isle of Wight.

- **DTI South East (Reigate)**
  Douglas House
  London Road
  Reigate
  Surrey
  RH2 9QP

  Tel: 0737 226900
  Fax: 0737 223491

  Covers Kent, Surrey, East and West Sussex.

- **DTI East**
  Building A
  Westbrook Centre
  Milton Road
  Cambridge
  CB4 1YG

  Tel: 0223 461939
  Fax: 0223 461941

Covers Norfolk, Suffolk, Essex, Cambridgeshire, Bedfordshire and Hertfordshire.

- **DTI North East**
Stanegate House
2 Groat Market
Newcastle-upon-Tyne
NE1 1YN
Tel: 091 232 4722
Fax: 091 232 6742
Serves Northumberland, Tyne and Wear, Cleveland, Durham.

- **DTI North West**
Sunley Tower
Piccadilly Plaza
Manchester
M1 4BA
Tel: 061 838 5000
Fax: 061 838 5236
Serves Cheshire, Lancashire, Merseyside, Greater Manchester, Cumbria, High Peak District of Derbyshire.

- **DTI North West (Liverpool)**
Graeme House
Derby Square
Liverpool
L2 7UP
Tel: 051 227 4111
Fax: 051 236 1140

- **DTI Yorkshire and Humberside**
25 Queen Street
Leeds
LS1 2TW
Tel: 0532 443171
Fax: 0532 338301/2
Serves North, South and West Yorkshire, Humberside.

- **DTI East Midlands**
Severns House
20 Middle Pavement
Nottingham
NG1 7DW
Tel: 0602 506181
Fax: 0602 587074
Serves Nottinghamshire, Derbyshire (except High Peak District), Leicestershire, Lincolnshire, Northamptonshire.

- **DTI West Midlands**
77 Paradise Circus
Queensway
Birmingham
B1 2DT
Tel: 021 212 5000
Fax: 021 212 1010
Serves Staffordshire, Warwickshire, Hereford and Worcester, Shropshire and West Midlands.

- **DTI South West**
The Pithay
Bristol
BS1 2PB
Tel: 0272 272666
Fax: 0272 299494
Serves Somerset, Wiltshire, Gloucestershire, Avon, Dorset.

- **DTI South West (Plymouth)**
Pheonix House
Notte Street
Plymouth
Devon
PL1 2HS
Tel: 0752 221891
Fax: 0752 227647
Serves Cornwall (including the Isles of Scilly), Devon.

- **Scottish Office**
Scottish Trade International
Franborough House
120 Bothwell Street
Glasgow
G2 7JP
Tel: 041 248 2700
Fax: 041 221 3712

- **Welsh Office**
Industry Department
Crown Building
Cathays Park
Cardiff
CF1 3NQ
Tel: 0222 825111
Fax: 0222 823088

## USEFUL ADDRESSES · 197

- **Northern Ireland**
  Industrial Development Board
  (Export Development Branch:
  Marketing Development
  Division)
  IDB House
  64 Chichester Street
  Belfast
  BT1 4JX
  Tel: 0232 233233
  Fax: 0232 231328

- **For information on assisted consultancy in Scotland and Wales contact:**

  **Enterprise Services Scotland Ltd**
  Apex 1
  99 Haymarket Terrace
  Edinburgh
  EH12 5EZ
  Tel: 031 313 6200
  Fax: 031 313 2378

**Welsh Development Agency**
Enterprise Initiative Unit
Business Development Centre
Treforest Industrial Estate
Mid-Glamorgan
CF37 5UR
Tel: 0443 841200
Fax: 0443 841121

### Country Desks (*Multi-country enquiries*)

- **Western Europe**
  Tel: 071 215 4786/4782/5336
  Fax: 071 215 5674

- **Belgium, Luxembourg, The Netherlands**
  Tel: 071 215 4794/5486
  (consumer goods);
  071 215 4790 (capital goods)
  Fax: 071 215 5071

- **Germany**
  Tel: 071 215 4795
  (consumer goods);
  071 215 4796 (capital goods)
  Fax: 071 215 5071

- **Austria, Switzerland, Liechtenstein**
  Tel: 071 215 4359
  Fax: 071 215 5674

- **Sweden, Norway, Denmark**
  Tel: 071 215 4397/5140
  Fax: 071 215 5674

- **Finland, Iceland**
  Tel: 071 215 5134
  Fax: 071 215 5674

- **Republic of Ireland**
  Tel: 071 215 4786/4782
  Fax: 071 215 5674

- France, Monaco
  Tel: 071 215 4762/4765
  (consumer goods);
  071 215 5197/5451 (capital goods)
  Fax: 071 215 5611

- **Italy, San Marino, Greece, Portugal, The Azores, Madeira**
  Tel: 071 215 5103
  (consumer goods);
  071 215 4776/4385 (capital goods)
  Fax: 071 215 5611

- **Spain, Andorra, Gibraltar, Canary Islands**
  Tel: 071 215 5624/5307
  (consumer goods);
  071 215 4284/8635
  (capital goods)
  Fax: 071 215 5611

# THE KNOW-HOW APPENDIX

## European Information Centres (EuroInfoCentres)

EuroInfoCentres can supply companies with information on all aspects of Community affairs, its policies, regulations and prospects.

- **Scotland**
  EuroInfoCentre Ltd
  Atrium Court
  3rd Floor
  50 Waterloo Street
  Glasgow
  G2 6HQ
  *Contact: Ian Traill*
  Tel: 041 221 0999
  Fax: 041 221 6539

  Highland Opportunity Ltd
  Development Department
  Highland Regional Council
  Glenurquhart Road
  Inverness
  IV3 5NX
  Tel: 0463 702560
  Fax: 0463 710848

  EuroInfoCentre
  20 Bridge Street
  Inverness
  *Contact: Norma Macdonald*
  Tel: 0463 702560
  Fax: 0463 715600

- **Wales**
  Wales EuroInfoCentre Ltd
  UWCC
  Guest Building
  PO Box 430
  Cardiff
  CF1 3XT
  *Contact: Brian Wilcox*
  Tel: 0222 229525
  Fax: 0222 229740
  or:
  *Eric Davies*
  Tel: 0352 704743
  Fax: 0352 753662

- **Northern Ireland**
  Local Enterprise Development Unit
  LEDU House
  Upper Galwally
  Belfast
  BT8 4TB
  *Contact: Eleanor Butterwick*
  Tel: 0232 491031
  Fax: 0232 691432

  Department of Economic Development
  Industrial Science Division
  17 Antrim Road
  Lisburn
  BT28 3AL
  *Contact: Rosie Goodwin*
  Tel: 0846 665161
  Fax: 0846 676054

  Industrial Development Board for Northern Ireland
  IDB House
  64 Chichester Street
  Belfast
  BT1 4JX
  *Contact: Jenny Graham*
  Tel: 0232 233233
  Fax: 0232 231328

- **England**
  EuroInfoCentre North of England
  Northern Development Company
  Great North House
  Sandyford Road
  Newcastle Upon Tyne
  NE1 8ND
  *Contact: Marion Schooler*
  Tel: 091 261 0026
  Fax: 091 222 1779

  EuroInfoCentre North West
  Liverpool City Libraries
  William Brown Street
  Liverpool
  L3 8EW
  *Contact: Howard Patterson*
  Tel: 051 298 1928
  Fax: 051 207 1342

  Manchester Chamber of Commerce and Industry
  56 Oxford Street
  Manchester
  M60 7JH

## USEFUL ADDRESSES • 199

*Contact: Sharon Quinlan*
Tel: 061 236 3210
Fax: 061 236 4160

EuroInfo Network Yorkshire and Humberside
Yorkshire and Humberside Development Association
Westgate House
100 Wellington Street
Leeds
LS1 4LT
*Contact: Christine Kenyon*
Tel: 0532 439222
Fax: 0532 431088

EuroBusiness InfoCentre West Yorkshire
West Yorkshire European Business Information Centre
Economic Development Centre
Britannia House
Broadway
Bradford
BD1 1JF
Contact: Jenny Lawson
Tel: 0274 754262
Fax: 0274 393226

Humberside European Business Information Centre
Hull University
Brynmor Jones Library
Cottingham Road
Hull
HU6 7RX
*Contact: Emma Theakston*
Tel: 0482 465940
Fax: 0482 466205

Mid Yorkshire European Information Centre
Leeds Metropolitan University Library
Calverley Street
Leeds
LS1 3HE
*Contact: John Chillag*
Tel: 0532 833126
Fax: 0532 833123

South Yorkshire European Information Centre
Sheffield Hallam University Library
Pond Street
Sheffield
S1 1WB
*Contact: Grahame Willis*
Tel: 0742 532126
Fax: 0742 532125

EuroInfoCentre Leicester
The Business Centre
10 York Road
Leicester
LE1 5TS
*Contact: Jeff Miller*
Tel: 0533 559944
Fax: 0533 553470

EuroInfoCentre Nottingham
Nottinghamshire Chamber of Commerce
The Business Advice Centre
309 Haydn Road
Nottingham
NG5 1DG
*Contact: Anne Pearce*
Tel: 0602 624624
Fax: 0602 856612

EuroInfoCentre Birmingham
Chamber of Commerce and Industry
PO Box 360
75 Harborne Road
Edgbaston
Birmingham
B15 3DH
*Contact: Sharon Clift*
Tel: 021 454 6171
Fax: 021 455 8670

EuroInfoCentre Shropshire and Staffordshire
Shropshire Chamber of Industry and Commerce
Industry House
Halesfield 20
Telford
Shropshire
TF7 4TA
*Contact: Stephanie Keates*
Tel: 0952 588766
Fax: 0952 582503

Staffordshire European
Business Centre
Staffordshire Development
Association
3 Martin Street
Stafford
ST16 2LH
*Contact: Stephanie Keates*
Tel: 0785 59528
Fax: 0785 21586

EuroInfoCentre Bristol
Bristol Chamber of Commerce
and Industry
16 Clifton Park
Clifton
Bristol
BS8 3BY
*Contact: Sarah Harris*
Tel: 0272 737373
Fax: 0272 745365

EuroInfoCentre South West
Exeter Enterprises Limited
Reed Hall
University of Exeter
Devon
EX4 4QR
*Contact: Diana Letcher*
Tel: 0392 214085
Fax: 0392 264375

EuroInfoCentre Brighton
Federation of Sussex
Industries (FSI) and Chamber
of Commerce and Industry
169 Church Road
Hove
East Sussex
BN3 2AS
*Contact: Benedicke Noakes*
Tel: 0273 26282
Fax: 0273 207965

EuroInfoCentre London
Centre for European Business
Information
Second Floor
11 Belgrave Road
London
SW1V 1RB
*Contact: Elizabeth Holmes*
Tel: 071 828 6201
Fax: 071 834 8416

EuroInfoCentre London
London Chamber of
Commerce
69 Cannon Street
London
EC4N 5AB
*Contact: Beth Rayney Cuday*
Tel: 071 489 1992
Fax: 071 489 0391

EuroInfoCentre Kent
County Hall
Maidstone
Kent
ME14 1XQ
*Contact: David Oxlade*
Tel: 0622 694109
Fax: 0622 691418

EuroInfoCentre Thames
Valley
Commerce House
2–6 Bath Road
Slough
SL1 3SB
*Contact: Julie Rees*
Tel: 0753 577877
Fax: 0753 524644

EuroInfoCentre – Southern
Area
Civic Centre
Southampton
SO9 4XP
*Contact: David Dance*
Tel: 0703 832866
Fax: 0703 231714

Isle of Wight Development
Board
EuroInfoCentre
Bugle House
117–118 High Street
Newport
Isle of Wight
PO30 1TP
Contact: Martin Lloyd
Tel: 0983 826222
Fax: 0983 826365

EuroInfoCentre East Anglia
112 Barrack Street
Norwich
NR3 1UB
*Contact: Sarah Abercrombie*
Tel: 0345 023114
Fax: 0603 633032

## USEFUL ADDRESSES • 201

## British Embassies and Consulates in EC and EFTA countries

British Embassies and Consulates are a useful source of information about trading rules and conditions. Exporters in the UK are requested not to approach the Commercial Departments of Embassies and Consulates without first consulting their DTI regional office.

- **Austria**
  The British Embassy
  Jaurèsgasse 12
  A–1030 VIENNA

  Tel: 010 431 7131575/9
  Fax: 010 431 757824

- **Belgium**
  The British Embassy
  rue d'Arlon/Arlonstraat 85
  1040 BRUSSELS

  Tel: 010 322 287 6211
  Fax: 010 322 287 6240
  Telex: 22703 (22703 BRITEM B)

- **Denmark**
  The British Embassy
  Kastelsveg 36/38/40
  DK–2100 COPENHAGEN

  Tel: 010 4531 264100
  Fax: 010 4535 431400

- **Finland**
  The British Embassy
  Itainen Puistotie 17
  00140 HELSINKI

  Tel: 010 3580 661293
  Fax: 010 3580 661342

- **France**
  The British Embassy
  35 rue du Faubourg St. Honoré
  75383 PARIS
  Cedex 08

  Tel: 010 331 42669142
  Fax: 010 331 42669590

  British Consulate General
  353 Boulevard du President Wilson, BP91
  33020 Bordeaux Cedex

  Tel: 010 33 56 42 34 13
  Fax: 010 33 56 08 33 12

  British Consulate General
  11 Square Dutilleul
  59800 Lille

  Tel: 010 33 20 57 87 90
  Fax: 010 33 20 54 88 16

  British Consulate General
  24 rue Childebert
  69002 Lyons Cedex 1

  Tel: 010 33 78 37 59 67
  Fax: 010 33 72 40 25 24

  British Consulate General
  24 Avenue du Prado
  13006 Marseilles

  Tel: 010 33 91 53 43 32
  Fax: 010 33 91 37 47 06

- **Germany**
  The British Embassy
  Friedrich-Ebert-Allée 77
  5300 BONN

  Tel: 010 49 228 234061
  Fax: 010 42 228 234070/237058

  Düsseldorf is the main commercial post and central point for UK trade promotion work in FRG.

  British Consulate General and Directorate of
  Trade Investment Promotion
  Yorck Strasse 19
  4000 Düsseldorf 30

  Tel: 010 49 211 9448222
  Fax: 010 49 211 486359

British Embassy (Berlin Office)
Commercial Section
IHZ Funktionsgebäude
Georgenstrasse 35
0-1086 Berlin

Tel: 010 49 30 2643 1680
Fax: 010 49 30 2643 1686

British Consulate-General
Triton Haus
Bockenheimer Landstrasse 42
W-6000 Frankfurt 1

Tel: 010 49 69 1700020
Fax: 010 49 69 72 95 53

British Consulate-General
Harvestehuder Weg 8A
2000 Hamburg 13

Tel: 010 49 40 44 60 71
Fax: 010 49 40 410 7259

British Consulate-General
Amalienstrasse 62
8000 Munich 40

Tel: 010 49 89 3816280
Fax: 010 49 89 331848

British Consulate-General
Breite Strasse 2
7000 Stuttgart 1

Tel: 010 49 711 16269-0
Fax: 010 49 711 16269-30

- **Greece**
  The British Embassy
  1 Ploutarchou Street
  GR–106 75 ATHENS

  Tel: 010 301 7236211
  Fax: 010 301 7241872

- **Iceland**
  The British Embassy
  Lanfasvegur 49
  101 Reykjavik
  PO Box 460
  121 Reykjavik

  Tel: 010 3541 15883–4
  Fax: 010 3541 27940

- **Ireland (Republic of)**
  The British Embassy
  31/33 Merrion Road
  DUBLIN 4

  Tel: 010 3531 2695211
  Fax: 010 3531 2838423

- **Italy**
  The British Embassy
  Via XX Settembre 80a
  00187 ROMA

  Tel: 4825441/4825551
  Fax: 4873324

  Milan is the main commercial post and central point for UK trade promotion work in Italy.

  British Consulate General
  Via San Paolo 7
  20121 Milan

  Tel: 010 392 8693442/3446
  Fax: 010 392 7202 0153

  British Embassy
  Via XX Settembre 80A
  00187 Rome

  Tel: 010 396 482 5441/5551
  Fax: 010 396 487 3324

  British Consulate
  Palazzo Casebarco
  Lungarno Corsini 2
  50123 Florence

  Tel: 010 3955 289556
  Fax: 010 39 55 219 112

  British Consulate General
  Via Francesco Crispi 122
  80122 Naples

  Tel: 010 3981 663511
  Fax: 010 3981 76 13720

  British Consulate
  Accademia
  Dorsoduro 1051
  Venice

  Tel: 010 3941 5227207/5227408
  Fax: 010 3941 9222617

  British Consulate
  Via XII Ottobre 2/131
  16121 Genoe

Tel: 010 39 10 564 833-6
Fax: 010 39 10 553 1516

British Consulate
Corso Massimo d'Azeglio 60
10126 Turin

Tel: 010 3911 687832/683921
Fax: 010 39 11 6699848

- **Liechtenstein**
Enquiries should be made to
the British Consulate General
in ZURICH

- **Luxembourg**
The British Embassy
14 Boulevard Roosevelt
PO Box 874
LUXEMBOURG

Tel: 010 352 229864/5/6
Fax: 010 352 229867

- **The Netherlands**
The British Embassy
Lange Voorhout 10
2514 ED
The Hague

Tel: 010 3170 364 5800
Fax: 010 3170 360 3839

- **Norway**
The British Embassy
Thomas Heftyesgate 8
0244 OSLO 2

Tel: (02) 552400
Fax: (02) 551041

- **Portugal**
The British Embassy
35–37 Rua de S Domingos a
Lapa
1200 LISBON

Tel: 010 3511 3961191/
3961147/3963181
Fax: 010 3511 3976768

British Consulate
Avenida da Boavista 3072
4100 Oporto

Tel: 010 3512 684789
Fax: 010 3512 6100 438

## USEFUL ADDRESSES · 203

- **Spain**
The British Embassy
Calle de Fernando el Santo 16
28010 MADRID

Tel: 010 341 319 0200
Fax: 010 341 319 419 0423

British Consulate General
Edificio Torre de Barcelona
Avenida Diagonal 477-13°
Barcelona 08036

Tel: 010 343 419 9044
Fax: 010 343 405 2411

British Consulate General
Alameda de Urquijo 2-8°
Bilbao 48008

Tel: 010 344 415 7600/7711/
7722
Fax: 010 344 416 7632

British Consulate
Plaza Nueva, 8, Dpdo
Seville 41001

Tel: 010 3454 228875
Fax: 010 3454 210323

British Consulate
Edificio Cataluña
PO Box 2020
c/. Luis Morote 6 - Third Floor
Puerto de la Luz
35007 - Las Palmas

Tel: 010 34 28 26 25 08
Fax: 010 34 28 267774

- **Sweden**
The British Embassy
Skarpögatan 6–8
115 27 STOCKHOLM

Tel: 010 468 6670140
Fax: 010 468 6629989

British Consulate General
Götgatan 15
41105 Gothenburg

Tel: 010 46 31 151 327
Fax: 010 46 31 15 3618

- **Switzerland**
The British Embassy
Thunstrasse 50
3005 BERNE 15

Tel: 010 4131 445021/6
Fax: 010 4131 440583

British Consulate General
Directorate of British Export
Promotion in
Switzerland
Dufourstrasse 56
8008 Zürich
Tel: 010 411 26 11 520
Fax: 010 411 252 8351

British Consulate General
37/39 rue de Vermont (6th Floor)
1211 Geneva 20
Tel: 010 4122 7343800
Fax: 010 4122 734 5254

## International chambers of commerce

The International Chambers of Commerce are an important source of local knowledge for firms trading with another member state.

- **Belgo-Luxembourg Chamber of Commerce in Great Britain**
  6 John Street
  London WC1N 2ES
  *Contact*: Peter Roscow
  Tel: 071 831 3508
  Fax: 071 831 9151
  *Sectors covered*: all
  *Restrictions on services*: higher rates for non-members
  *Information and advice offered*
  General: market statistics, marketing, exporting, finding an agent (in Belgium and Luxembourg only)
  Company specific: strategic advice, individual counselling

- **French Chamber of Commerce in Great Britain**
  2nd Floor
  Knightsbridge House
  197 Knightsbridge
  London SW7 1RB
  *Contact*: Genevieve Brulet
  Tel: 071 225 5254
  Fax: 071 225 5557
  *Sectors covered*: all
  *Restrictions on services*: discretionary charges for non-members
  *Information and advice offered*
  General: list of French importers/exporters, translation, market research, finding an agent (for France only)
  Company specific: individual counselling, strategic advice

- **German Chamber of Industry and Commerce in the UK**
  16 Buckingham Gate
  London SW1E 6LB
  *Contact*: Klaus Balzer
  Tel: 071 233 5656
  Fax: 071 233 7835
  *Sectors covered*: all
  *Restrictions on services*: non-members charged for services
  *Information and advice offered*
  General: marketing, legal advice, tax advice, exporting, finding an agent (all for Germany only), bad debt recovery
  Company specific: strategic advice, individual counselling

- **Italian Chamber of Commerce for Great Britain**
  Walmar House
  296 Regent Street
  London W1R 6AE
  *Contact*: Franco Pace
  Tel: 071 637 3062
  Fax: 071 436 6037
  *Sectors covered*: all
  *Restrictions on services*: only initial advice free to non-members

## USEFUL ADDRESSES • 205

*Information and advice offered*
General: market research, finding an agent, organisation of conferences
Company specific: status reports on Italian companies and sole traders

- **Netherlands–British Chamber of Commerce**
  The Dutch House
  307–308 High Holborn
  London WC1V 7LS

  *Contact*: S Rex Kingsley
  Tel: 071 405 1358
  Fax: 071 405 1689

  *Sectors covered*: all

  *Restrictions on services*: only initial advice free to non-members

  *Information and advice offered*
  General: exporting, finding an agent, market research (all for Netherlands only), publications
  Company specific: marketing in the Netherlands

- **Norwegian Chamber of Commerce, London Inc**
  Norway House
  21–24 Cockspur Street
  London SW1Y 5BN

  Tel: 071 930 0181
  Fax: 071 930 7946

- **Portuguese UK Chamber of Commerce**
  4th Floor
  22/25A Sackville Street
  London W1X 1DE

  *Contact*: Ronald Price
  Tel: 071 494 1844
  Fax: 071 494 1822

  *Sectors covered*: all

  *Restrictions on services*: only basic advice free to non-members

  *Information and advice offered*
  General: marketing, market research, market statistics, exporting, finding an agent, joint ventures, publications, conferences (all in Portugal)
  Company specific: individual counselling and support services

- **Spanish Chamber of Commerce in Great Britain**
  5 Cavendish Square
  London W1M 0DP

  *Contact*: Nicolas Belmonte
  Tel: 071 637 9061
  Fax: 071 436 7188

  *Sectors covered*: all

  *Restrictions on services*: preference given to members

  *Information and advice offered*
  General: market research, market statistics (Spain only), finding an agent (members only), guidance on Spanish legislation
  Company specific: individual counselling service

- **Swedish Chamber of Commerce for the UK**
  72/73 Welbeck Street
  London W1M 7HA

  Tel: 071 486 4545
  Fax: 071 935 5487

## European Commission Information Offices

European Commission Information Offices can signpost businesses to sources of European information. A full collection of EC papers and legislation can be inspected in office libraries.

- **England**
  Jean Monnet House
  8 Storey's Gate
  London SW1P 3AT
  Tel: 071 973 1992
  Fax: 071 979 1900/1910

## 206 • THE KNOW-HOW APPENDIX

- **Scotland**
  9 Alva Street
  Edinburgh
  EH2 4PH
  Contact: Diane Hart
  Tel: 031 225 2058
  Fax: 031 226 4105

- **Northern Ireland**
  Windsor House
  9–15 Bedford Street
  Belfast
  BT2 7EG
  Tel: 0232 240708
  Fax: 0232 248241

- **Wales**
  4 Cathedral Road
  Cardiff
  CF1 9SG
  Tel: 0222 371631
  Fax: 0222 395489

- **European Parliament UK Information Office**
  (Provides general information and documentation on the Parliament's proceedings)
  2 Queen Anne's Gate
  London SW1H 9AA
  Tel: 071 222 0411
  Fax: 071 222 2713

## Publishers of national legislation

- **Austria**
  (*Bundesgesetzblatt für die Republik Österreich* (Federal Law Gazette for the Republic of Austria))
  Österreichische Staatsdruckerei
  Rennweg 12a
  A–1037 VIENNA

- **Belgium**
  (*Moniteur Belge/Belgisch Staatsblad* (Belgian Monitor))
  Direction du Moniteur Belge
  rue de Louvain 40–42
  1000 BRUSSELS

- **Denmark**
  (*Lovtidende for Kongeriget Danmark* (Law Gazette of the Kingdom of Denmark))
  Justitsministeriet
  Slotsholmsgade 10
  1216 COPENHAGEN K

- **Finland**
  (*Suomen Laki I–II* (Code of Finnish Law))
  Lakimiestliiton Kustannus
  Undermaankatu 4–6
  SF–00120 HELSINKI

- **France**
  (*Journal Officiel de la Republic Francaise* (Official Gazette of the French Republic))
  Direction des Journaux Officiels
  26 rue Desaix
  75727 PARIS

- **Germany**
  (*Bundesanzeiger* (Federal Gazette))
  Bundesanzeiger-Verlag GmbH
  Breit Strasse
  78–80 Postfach 108006
  D–5000 KÖLN

- **Greece**
  (*Efèmeris tês Kubernêsôs tês Ellenikês Demokratias* (Government Gazette of the Greek Republic))
  Ethnikon Tupografeion
  25 Kapodistriou Street
  10432 ATHENS

- **Iceland**
  (*Lögbirtingablad* (Official Gazette))
  Skrifstofa Bladsins
  Langaveg 1
  REYKJAVIK

- **Ireland**
  (*Na Hachtanna der Oireachtas* (The Acts of the Oireachtas))

Government Publications Sale Office
Sun Alliance House
Molesworth Street
DUBLIN 2

- **Italy**
(*Gazzetta Ufficiale Della Repubblica Italiana* (Official Gazette of the Italian Republic))

Instituo Poligraphico e zecca delle Stato (IPZS)
Piazza Verdi 10
00100 ROMA

- **Luxembourg**
(*Memorial, Journal Officiel du Grand-Duche de Luxembourg* (Official Gazette of the Grand-Duchy of Luxembourg))

Service Central de Législation
10 Boulevard Roosevelt
2910 LUXEMBOURG

- **The Netherlands**
(*Nederlandse Staatscourant* (Netherlands Government Gazette))

Staatsuitgeverij
Christoffel Plantifristratt 2
Postbus 20014
2500 EA
The Hague

- **Norway**
(*Norsk Lortidend* (Norwegian Law Gazette))

Gröndahl and Sön Forlag
PO Box 2308
Solli 0201
OSLO 2

- **Portugal**
(*Boletim do Ministério da Justiça* (Bulletin of the Ministry of Justice (Supplement: Legislation))

Ministerio da Justiça
Gabinete de Gestao Financeira
Praçd do Comércio
1194 LISBON CEDEX

- **Spain**
(*Boletin Oficial del Estado* (Official Bulletin of the State))

Boletin Oficial del Estado
Calle Trafalgar 29
28010 MADRID

- **Sweden**
(*Svensk Författningssamling* (Swedish Code of Statutes))

Allmänna Förlaget
Kundtjänst
10647 STOCKHOLM

- **Switzerland**
(*Bundesblatt* (Official Gazette))

Eldgenössische Drucksachen- und Materialzentrale (EDMZ)
Gruppe Buchhandel und Werbung
Fellerstrasse 21
3000 BERN

- **United Kingdom**
(Her Majesty's Stationery Office)

HMSO Books
49 High Holborn
LONDON
WC1

## 1.5 Useful publications

DTI publications may be obtained by ringing the Business in Europe Hotline on 0272 444888:

- *The Single Market: The Facts* gives details of the Community's programme for completing the single market and lists the measures planned and those adopted at the time of going to press.
- *Trading within Europe*

- *European Economic Area*
- *Breaking through the Barriers*
- *Progress on Commission White Paper* copies available from 071 215 4647.
- *Spearhead: The easy-to-use guide to EC legislation*, gives information about Spearhead, the DTI's on-line database of single market information.
- *Guide to sources of advice*
- *'Brussels can you hear me?' Influencing decisions in the European Community.*
- *Europe open for professions*
- *Guide to public purchasing*
- *Financial Services*
- *Company law harmonisation*
- *Merger Control in Europe.* Copies available from 071 215 6828.
- *Keeping your product on the market* explains the New Approach to technical harmonisation and how firms can influence the standards-making process. There is also a series of booklets on individual 'New Approach' directives:
  * *Conformity Assessment.*
  * *Preventing new technical barriers.*
  * *Simple pressure vessels – UK Regulations.*
  * *Toy Safety – UK Regulations.*
  * *Electromagnetic compatibility.*
  * *Construction products – UK Regulations.*
  * *Machinery*
  * *Personal protective equipment.*
  * *Non-automatic weighing instruments.*
  * *Gas appliances.*
  * *Active implantable medical devices.*
  * *Medical devices.*
  * *Telecommunications terminal equipment.*
  * *Equipment for use in potentially explosive atmospheres.*

## Other publications

*Directory of the Commission* (available from HMSO (071 873 9090)), is published periodically and lists senior officials in the Commission services.

*Vacher's European Companion and Consultants' Register* (published quarterly), contains information about Community institutions and other European and international organisations and a useful list of contacts. (Available from Vacher's Publications, 113 High Street, Berkhamsted, Herts HP4 2DJ. Tel: 0442 876135).

*The European Companion 1992* (published by Dod's), is a guide to the EC and those who work in it. It contains biographies and photographs of leading EC politicians and personnel and describes the structure, function and role of the main institutions.

## 1.6 Other contacts

- **The Law Society's Information Office**
  50 Chancery Lane
  London WC2A 1SX
  Tel: 071 320 5688

- **The Law Society of Northern Ireland**
  Law Society House
  98 Victoria Street
  Belfast BT1 3JZ
  Tel: 0232 231614
  Fax: 0232 232606

- **The Law Society of Scotland**
  The Law Society's Hall
  26 Drumsheugh Gardens
  Edinburgh EH3 7YR
  Tel: 031 226 7411 Ext. 253
  Fax: 031 225 2934

- **HMSO**
  51 Nine Elms Lane
  London SW8 5DR
  Tel: 071 873 8409
  (subscriptions to agency titles, including EC official journals);
  071 873 8499 (subscriptions to HMSO titles); 071 873 9090
  (general ordering service)

- **HMSO sub-agent**
  Dawson UK Ltd
  Canon House
  Folkestone
  Kent CT19 5EE
  Tel: 0303 850101

- **World Aid Section**
  Department of Trade and Industry
  Room 123
  Ashdown House
  123 Victoria Street
  London SW1E 6RB
  Tel: (projects in Europe)
  071 215 6157
  Tel: (projects elsewhere)
  071 215 6765

- **The Single Market Compliance Unit**
  Department of Trade and Industry
  Room 602
  Ashdown House
  123 Victoria Street
  London SW1E 6RB
  Tel: 071 215 6730/5610
  Fax: 071 222 5226

# II · The EUROPEAN ECONOMIC AREA

## II.1 What is the European Economic Area Agreement?

The aim of the European Economic Area (EEA) Agreement is to strengthen trade and economic relations between the European Community (EC) and the European Free Trade Association (EFTA: Austria, Finland, Iceland, Liechtenstein, Norway, Sweden and Switzerland).

*Only six of the seven member states of EFTA are to participate in the EEA; Switzerland has declined to participate. As a result of the Swiss decision to remain outside the EEA, the term 'EFTA' where used in this text in the context of the EEA, should be understood to mean those members of EFTA which are contracting parties to the EEA Agreement (i.e. not Switzerland).*

The EEA Agreement, which effectively extends the single market to EFTA, covers the free movement of goods, services, capital and people and rules on competition and state aids. The Agreement also provides for enhanced co-operation on 'flanking policies' such as the environment and research and development. The EFTA states will take on relevant Community legislation and establish new institutions to ensure that the EEA rules, particularly those on competition and state aids, are observed.

### When and how will the EEA Agreement be implemented?

The EEA Agreement was signed on 2 May 1992 and would have entered into force on 1 January 1993, the same date set for completion of the single market, if ratified by then by all Community and EFTA member states. However, following a referendum in December 1992, Switzerland has decided not to participate. As a result the EEA Agreement will not now extend to Switzerland.

The Community and the rest of EFTA remain committed to the EEA and work is currently underway to identify the revisions to the agreement necessary to reflect Switzerland's decision not to join. It is hoped that these amendments can be agreed at a diplomatic conference early in 1993, after which contracting parties will need to ratify the amended Agreement. It should be noted that the need for Liechtenstein to renegotiate its customs union with Swizerland may result in Liechtenstein acceding to the EEA shortly after it comes into force in other contracting states.

In the UK, the EEA Bill, which gives effect to the UK's obligations under the EEA Agreement, was introduced into the House of Commons on 25 November 1992, having passed through all its stages in the House of Lords. In an answer to a Parliamentary Question on 8 December 1992 the President of the Board of Trade stated that the government would announce how to proceed with the EEA Bill when the impact of the Swiss decision not to participate in the EEA had been fully assessed.

The UK strongly supports the creation of the EEA and hopes that it will be possible to bring a revised Agreement into force as soon as possible.

## Background

The EC and EFTA are already significant trading partners and have a long history of co-operation.

The first major step was the conclusion of the EC/EFTA Free Trade Agreements in 1972–73. These abolished tariffs and quotas for trade in industrial goods, and in a limited range of processed agricultural products, between the EC and the EFTA countries, allowing trade between the two areas to flourish. In 1990, 10 per cent of all EC exports were to EFTA countries: representing 61 per cent of EFTA's total imports. The EC has become a crucial market for EFTA's goods: taking as much as 58 per cent of EFTA exports in the same year (10 per cent of total EC imports).

While the Free Trade Agreements represented a significant advance in free trade between the two areas, a number of important non-tariff barriers to trade remained. Furthermore, the Agreements were only concerned with free movement of goods; they made no provision for the free movement of services, capital or persons, all of which are necessary to a genuinely free market.

At a meeting in Luxembourg in 1984, EC and EFTA ministers agreed that it would be beneficial for both areas to move towards a closer relationship: and the idea of the EEA was born. Following this, the two areas started to co-operate actively in a number of areas, such as standardisation procedures, simplified trading procedures and research and development. However, it was soon realised that there was a limit to what could be achieved on an informal basis and that a more formal and wide-ranging structure was required.

The idea of the EEA in its current form was proposed early in 1989. After lengthy and complex negotiations between the EC and EFTA, which started in June 1990, the EEA Agreement was finally signed in May 1992. As noted above, Switzerland decided, in a referendum on 6 December 1992, not to participate in the EEA. As a result, trade between the Community and Switzerland will continue to be governed by the terms of the 1972 Free Trade Agreement. The consequences for Liechtenstein, which participates in that Agreement through its 1923 Customs Union with Switzerland, remain to be worked out.

## Main features of the EEA Agreement

The main features of the EEA Agreement are as follows:

- the 'four freedoms' of the EC – free movement of goods, services, capital and persons – will apply throughout the EEA. EFTA countries will adopt almost all the EC single market legislation;
- an EEA regime on competition and state aids, based on existing EC rules, will aim to ensure competitive conditions of trade throughout the Area;
- there will be closer co-operation between the EC and EFTA in a number of key areas such as research and development, the environment and education;

## WHAT IS THE EUROPEAN ECONOMIC AREA AGREEMENT? • 215

- EFTA will set up a new fund to assist some of the poorer regions of the Community, including Northern Ireland;
- new EEA institutions will be set up to administer the Agreement and ensure that both areas comply with its rules;
- it will be a dynamic agreement. The EFTA states will take on new single market measures as they are adopted by the EC and will have a chance to influence new proposals.

## Form of the Agreement

The EEA Agreement consists of over 500 pages. It has been published by HMSO as a Command Paper (Cm 2073). The main text of the Agreement contains its principal provisions, many of which correspond to provisions of the EEC Treaty. This is supplemented by 49 Protocols and 22 Annexes. The Protocols contain detailed provisions which apply to specific areas covered by the Agreement, such as rules of origin, competition and trade in fish. The Annexes list the EC measures which are to be adopted by EFTA; these amount to some 1,500 measures, or 12,000 pages of the *'acquis communautaire'* (the existing body of EC law).

The Agreement as signed contain only those measures which were adopted by the EC before 1 August 1991. However, there is provision for subsequent EC measures to be added to the Agreement on an ongoing basis. This process will start as soon as the Agreement comes into force.

Parallel Agreements have also been concluded between the EC and EFTA countries which cover specific issues relating to Alpine transit, fish and agricultural trade.

## Opportunities for the UK

The EFTA countries are already important trading partners for the UK. In 1991, trade with the EFTA countries accounted for 7 per cent of the UK's visible exports, amounting to a total value of £7.7 billion. Important export sectors include office machines and data processing equipment, electrical and other industrial machinery, manufactured goods, chemicals and transport equipment. However, there are undoubtedly many further opportunities in the EFTA markets for UK companies to exploit.

The EEA will make it easier for UK companies to do business in the EFTA countries, in the same way that the EC single market is opening up new opportunities in other countries within the EC. Most of the existing barriers to trade, which have hampered the performance of UK exporters and service suppliers, will be removed. This will certainly be welcomed by the many UK companies who are already trading with EFTA. It should also encourage many other UK companies to enter these affluent markets for the first time.

Of course, the EFTA countries will also enjoy the benefits of the EEA, as will other EC member states. EFTA companies will be better placed to compete with UK companies for business both in the UK and in other EC markets. Similarly, companies from other EC countries will also find it easier to do business in EFTA and will be actively competing with UK suppliers for the new opportunities in EFTA markets which the EEA Agreement will bring. UK companies should take both these factors into account in planning their marketing strategies. However, we believe that the increased opportunities for UK companies in EFTA should more than outweigh any adverse impact which might come from increased competition.

## II.2  Free movement of goods

The EEA will be a major step forward for free movement of goods between the EC and EFTA. The improvements are in three main areas:

- removal of non-tariff barriers to trade;
- further abolition and reductions of tariffs;
- simplification of trading procedures.

Unless otherwise specified, the free movement of goods provisions apply only to products originating in the EC and EFTA.

### Removal of non-tariff barriers

The most important improvement in the area of free movement of goods will be the elimination of some of the major non-tariff barriers to trade. The Agreement will introduce throughout the EEA:

- common technical and safety regulations;
- a ban on discriminatory taxation;
- an open public purchasing policy;
- controls over the commercial behaviour of state monopolies.

#### Technical and safety regulations
The EFTA countries will adopt most of the EC legislation which is concerned with technical and safety regulation. This will mean that products which meet those EC requirements will be able to circulate freely throughout the EEA. UK exporters will no longer have to comply with a different set of standards when producing products for the EFTA markets and UK products will no longer need to be tested in the EFTA countries once they have been approved in the UK.

Currently, technical regulations in the EFTA countries are often more complex than those of the EC and, in some sectors, are more demanding, quite apart from the fact that the various individual EFTA countries each have their own separate rules with which UK exporters have to comply.

The introduction of common regulations will make it easier for UK manufacturers to export to the EFTA countries and, for existing exporters to EFTA, should result in considerable savings in terms of time and cost. Many different sectors will benefit: such as motor vehicles (from 1 January 1995), household appliances, electrical equipment, food and drink, cosmetics, pharmaceuticals, chemicals and toys.

While the EEA introduces a common approach to standards throughout the area and mutual recognition of the standards of the various EEA member states, this does not mean that standards will be the same in all countries. For example, EFTA countries will still be able to specify stricter environmental standards for their own domestic vehicle manufacturers, even though they will not be able to use these to exclude vehicles from other EEA countries. However, while many differences remain, the EC and EFTA (including Switzerland, even though it will not participate in the EEA) have already made considerable progress towards harmonising technical standards via their participation in CEN (European Committee for Standardisation) and CENELEC (European Committee for Electrotechnical Standards) and this work will actively continue.

**Discriminatory taxation**
The EEA Agreement will ban the use of taxation to discriminate against goods coming from another country within the Area in order to protect local suppliers. A good example is spirits where some EFTA countries have imposed very high taxes on imports of UK products, such as Scotch whisky, in order to protect their own producers of local spirits. This will no longer be possible when the EEA is in force.

There will still be differences in the method and level of taxation between EEA countries. Unlike the EC, EFTA countries will not have to levy VAT and will continue to be free to set their own local tax and excise rates at whatever level they choose. However, it will not be possible for them to use taxation to give unfair protection to local products by penalising imported goods.

**Purchasing by public authorities and regulated utilities**
Public authorities and utilities (energy, transport, water and telecommunications) with special or exclusive rights (regulated utilities) have enormous purchasing power, with responsibility for awarding major contracts for the supply of a wide range of goods, works and services. The EFTA countries tend to have restrictive public purchasing policies which strongly favour local suppliers. It can be very difficult, if not impossible, for UK companies to compete in what is potentially a highly lucrative market.

The EEA Agreement will open up public purchasing in EFTA, as the EFTA countries will adopt the EC procurement Directives for works, supplies of goods and utilities in full. All public contracts and contracts awarded by regulated utilities for the procurement of goods and works above specified value thresholds will be subject to the terms of these Directives, in EFTA as well as in the EC. The services Directive (Directive on supply of services) is not yet included in the EEA. The Directives apply to all public bodies, both national and local, and to all publicly owned utilities, and utilities with special or exclusive rights.

This is a major step forward. It creates excellent new opportunities for UK companies in a number of key areas: such as construction, engineering, steel, office equipment, telecommunications, transport equipment and supplies for oil and gas exploration and development.

The new rules will apply in most EFTA countries as soon as the EEA Agreement comes into force. They will not apply in Liechtenstein until

1 January 1995. In addition, Norway will have until 1 January 1995 to implement the utilities procurement Directive.

### State monopolies

In some of the EFTA countries, state monopolies play an important role in controlling the commercial markets for widely consumed products such as alcohol, tobacco and salt. Their purchasing and marketing policies may tend to favour local producers and make it difficult for imports to compete.

Under the EEA Agreement, state monopolies of this type will no longer be allowed to pursue purchasing and marketing policies which discriminate against products from other EEA countries. Thus an EFTA monopoly will not be able to block the importation of a UK brand, or limit its distribution, in order to protect local products or its own trading activities.

## Abolition and reductions of tariffs and quotas

The EEA Agreement contains provision for the abolition of tariffs and quotas on a range of manufactured food and drink products which were not included in the Free Trade Agreements. Some important examples are whisky, beer, confectionery, soups, sauces and processed vegetables.

Tariffs on the imports of fish and fish products will be abolished or gradually phased out by both the EC and EFTA. However, certain 'sensitive species' will still be protected, where these are of particular national importance; for example, import tariffs will remain on salmon, mackerel and herring.

The Agreement does not cover unprocessed agricultural produce. EFTA will not join in the Common Agricultural Policy (CAP), which will remain unchanged. However, the EC and EFTA are committed to work towards liberalising agricultural trade over time. As a first step, the EC has signed separate agreements on agriculture with the EFTA countries, which will introduce mutual tariff and quota concessions on a limited range of produce.

## Simplified trading procedures

An important difference between the EC and the EEA is that the EEA is not a customs union. Both the EC and the EFTA states will still be free (within their respective GATT obligations) to set their own tariffs on goods coming from third countries and border controls between the EC and EFTA states (and between the EFTA states themselves) will still remain. However, the EEA Agreement takes steps to simplify trading procedures between the two areas and to reduce the necessary formalities, continuing the progress which has already been made in this area over the last few years.

The main points here are:

- *rules of origin*: the rules of origin have been simplified and improved. 'Full cumulation' has been introduced. This means that the value of any processing carried out in the EEA can now be added to the value of materials (raw materials or components, for example) which originate

in the EEA for the purposes of determining whether a product qualifies for EEA preferential origin treatment. There is also greater opportunity for including non-EEA materials or processing (normally up to 10 per cent). In addition, documentary procedures will be simplified.
- *customs formalities*: there will be random checks instead of universal inspection of vehicles at border crossings. Paperwork will be further reduced and there will be greater use of electronically transmitted documentation. Both areas have committed to closer co-operation between their customs authorities.
- *further simplification*: the EC and EFTA have agreed to work towards simplifying trading procedures still further and will co-operate closely to bring this about.

Again, the aim is to reduce barriers to trade between the two areas. These measures will help to make it easier to export to the EFTA countries and will result in savings of time and cost for UK exporters.

## 11.3 Free movement of services

The provisions of the EC/EFTA Free Trade Agreements did not cover the increasingly important service sector. Currently, there are a number of restrictions on the provision of services in the EFTA countries, some of which apply in important and profitable areas such as financial services where UK companies would be strongly placed to compete given the opportunity.

The EEA Agreement provides for the first time for free movement of services throughout the Area. Any company or individual established in an EEA country will be free to provide industrial, commercial or professional services throughout the Area under the same conditions which apply within the EC single market. In a number of important sectors – such as financial services, transport, audio-visual services, professional services and telecommunications – the EFTA states will take on the relevant EC rules, which will ensure a common approach throughout the EEA and will allow UK companies to compete on an equal footing with domestic suppliers.

This will be of benefit to a wide range of service industries. As an example, the banking sector will benefit from the extension of the second banking co-ordination Directive to the EEA. This will enable UK banks to establish branches throughout the EEA without having to seek separate authorisation in the host country, offering new opportunities in countries which have until now imposed restrictions on the operation of foreign banks on their territory.

UK providers of services will also benefit from the Agreement's provisions on the mutual recognition of professional qualifications.

## II.4 Right of establishment

As already described, the EEA Agreement will make it easier for UK companies to sell their goods and services in the EFTA countries. While some UK companies may choose to do this from a UK operating base, others may see advantages in setting up operations in the EFTA countries themselves. This too will be easier, as the Agreement introduces the 'right of establishment' for EEA nationals throughout the Area.

What this means is that EEA nationals, whether companies or individuals, may establish themselves for business purposes anywhere within the Area on the same terms as local businesses, free from any restrictions which do not apply to local businesses, unless there are overriding reasons for restrictions related to factors such as national security or public health. They will be able to:

- operate as self-employed individuals;
- set up and manage businesses under the same conditions as local individuals and companies; and
- set up local branches or subsidiaries.

To qualify as an 'EEA company' for these purposes, a company must be formed in accordance with the law of an EC or EFTA member state and must have its registered office, central administration or principal place of business within the EEA.

It will no longer be possible for EFTA countries, therefore, to discriminate against companies or individuals from elsewhere in the EEA who wish to set up businesses in their territory (for example, by refusing permission to operate in a particular sector by virtue of nationality or by imposing stringent conditions which do not apply to domestic firms).

## II.5 Free movement of persons

The EEA Agreement will make it easier for UK citizens to live and work in the EFTA countries and, equally, for UK companies to employ EFTA nationals.

The Agreement gives all EC and EFTA nationals the right to work throughout the EEA. They will be able to:

- accept offers of employment in any EEA country;
- stay in that country to work; and
- remain there afterwards (subject to certain status conditions).

This applies to all types of employment with the exception of certain jobs in the public sector.

Throughout the Area, EEA nationals must not be prevented from being hired and employed on the same terms as local workers. There can be no legal or other official discrimination between them, or between the nationals of different EEA countries, in respect of employment, pay or working conditions.

The right to reside anywhere within the EEA will also apply to the families of EEA migrant workers and to non-working EC and EFTA nationals, including students and retired people. However, there are restrictions on claiming public funds; people cannot move to another country if they would be a burden on the social security system there. Individuals may also be excluded on the grounds of public policy (such as morality), health and security.

Passport controls will still remain at EC/EFTA border crossings, but the EC and EFTA states have agreed to try to ease border control formalities for EEA nationals.

The Agreement provides for the mutual recognition of diplomas and other professional qualifications throughout the EEA. The EFTA countries will adopt all the main EC measures in this area including the general Directive on the mutual recognition of professional qualifications and a number of Directives which apply to specific professional sectors. This means that, for example, an engineer, doctor or architect qualified in the UK will be able to seek work in an EFTA country on the basis of his or her UK qualification. Similarly, UK companies will be able to recruit suitably qualified professionals from the EFTA countries.

The EFTA countries have agreed to adopt the provisions of the main EC social security Regulation for migrant workers, which will apply throughout the EEA once the Agreement is in force. This provides a means to co-ordinate benefit arrangements between countries and will ensure that EEA migrants are not disadvantaged, either in the host country or in their home country, as a result of working in another member state.

The provisions for free movement of persons will take effect in most of the EEA countries as soon as the Agreement is implemented. However, Liechtenstein has been allowed until 1998 to implement the provisions in full.

## 11.6 Free movement of capital

The Agreement will remove restrictions on the movement of capital belonging to EEA residents (both individuals and companies) within the EEA.

The main impact will be in the area of investment. Countries within the EEA will (with certain limited exceptions) not be able to restrict investment in a way which discriminates against individuals and companies from other EEA countries. They will not be allowed to retain investment rules which prohibit or limit investment from elsewhere in the EEA.

This again is a very important step forward, as the EFTA countries have traditionally tended to impose considerable restrictions on inward investment by foreign individuals and concerns. The removal of these restrictions will create significant new opportunities for UK investors and investment advisers. There will be many new possibilities in areas such as cross-border takeovers, mergers and joint ventures with EFTA companies and in the property market.

The Agreement should also help to attract increased inward investment from the EFTA countries which will benefit the UK economy.

Some barriers to investment will remain. For example, the financial structure of companies in some of the EFTA countries may limit the scope for foreign equity participation (this is also the case in some EC countries). However, it will not be possible for companies to maintain such structures with the deliberate aim of excluding foreign investors. The intention is to work towards breaking down these structural barriers over time.

Another important element in the Agreement is that most of the EC rules which govern the operation of the financial markets and co-operation between financial regulators in different member states will be adopted by EFTA. This will apply in areas such as stock market regulation.

Free movement of capital was a particularly sensitive area in the EEA negotiations, as its introduction will mean significant changes to the economic structure of many of the EFTA countries. It was therefore agreed that the full provisions would not take effect throughout the EEA immediately on implementation of the Agreement and a number of transitional periods have been allowed.

## II.7 Competition and state aids

A major achievement of the EEA Agreement is the introduction of common rules on competition and state aids throughout the Area.

Companies operating within the EC must comply with strict EC competition rules which are actively enforced by the European Commission. The situation in EFTA is very different. The EC/EFTA Free Trade Agreements contain similar rules to those in force in the EC. However, the content of competition law in EFTA countries and the method and effectiveness of its enforcement is often less stringent than in the EC.

The EEA Agreement aims to achieve a common approach by applying to the whole of the EEA rules similar to the EC's existing competition rules. Once the Agreement is in force, EFTA will be bound by equivalent rules concerned with:

- restrictive trading agreements;
- monopoly abuse;
- mergers and takeovers; and
- state aids.

EFTA will also be bound by the competition and state aids rules similar to those of the European Coal and Steel Community (ECSC).

The use of identical competition rules throughout the EEA, backed by effective provision for their enforcement, will play a major part in helping to create a 'level playing field' across the whole Area and is a crucial feature of the Agreement. Industry and commerce will benefit from both more equal conditions of competition and simpler, standardised procedures, while the consumer will benefit from the increased choice and lower prices which effective competition brings.

The adoption by the EFTA states of the strict EC rules on state aids will ensure that companies based in EFTA do not enjoy an unfair competitive advantage over EC-based companies. This will be of considerable benefit to UK companies operating in sectors such as steel, aircraft and vehicles which up until now have often been heavily subsidised in the EFTA countries.

### Competition authorities in the EEA

The European Commission, with the backing of the European Court of Justice (ECJ), will maintain its responsibility for enforcing the competition rules within the EC. In addition, a new body – the EFTA Surveillance Authority (ESA) – will be set up with responsibility for seeing that the rules are properly enforced within EFTA, backed by a new EFTA Court.

The ESA will have similar powers within the EFTA countries which are participating in the EEA to those which the European Commission now enjoys within the EC. The two Authorities will work closely together – and, when appropriate, with the competition authorities of member states – to ensure that the rules are properly enforced throughout the Area and that a common approach is maintained in the two areas.

The Agreement adopts a 'one-step shop' approach to EEA-wide competition cases where both the EC and EFTA are affected, which means that each case will be handled by only one Authority. It contains rules which determine which Authority will have responsibility.

## 11.8 Other common rules

EFTA will take on most of the main EC rules in a number of other important areas. These include:

- intellectual property;
- industrial and commercial property;
- company law (to be phased in over three years);
- the environment;
- consumer protection;
- energy;
- social policy;
- animal and plant health; and
- statistics.

## 11.9 Increased co-operation between the EC and EFTA

As well as extending the single market to EFTA, the Agreement aims to strengthen EC/EFTA links by providing for increased co-operation between the two areas in a number of important fields. These are:

- research and technology;
- information services;
- the environment;
- education, training and youth;
- social policy;
- consumer protection;
- small and medium-sized enterprises;
- tourism;
- the audio-visual sector; and
- civil protection.

Some of these – notably, research and technology – are areas in which the EC and EFTA have a long history of regular collaboration, while others represent a completely new development.

Within these selected fields, the EFTA states will be able to participate fully in major EC framework and action programmes, such as the third framework programme, which is concerned with research and technology. EFTA member states will make a full – and, probably, substantial – financial contribution to programme costs and will be represented on the committees which run the programmes.

As well as providing for collaboration within the formal programmes, the Agreement aims to encourage the EC and the EFTA states to set up other joint activities and to exchange information on a regular basis through both formal and informal channels.

Once the Agreement is in force, the EC and the EFTA states will be able to extend this framework for co-operation to other fields if they decide this would be of mutual benefit.

Under these new arrangements, the EC will derive considerable benefit from EFTA's high level of expertise in important areas such as high technology and the environment and, of course, from EFTA's financial contribution.

Finally, the Agreement also seeks to encourage:

- *political co-operation* between the two areas, both formally and informally;
- EC/EFTA dialogue on *economic and monetary policy*; and
- the development of comparable *statistics* on economic, social and environmental parameters.

# II.10 The EEA Financial Mechanism

The EFTA countries have agreed to set up a fund which will help the less-favoured regions of the EC. This will be known as the EEA Financial Mechanism, although it is sometimes referred to as the 'EFTA Cohesion Fund'.

Under the Agreement, EFTA was to have provided ECU 500 million in grants over five years and an interest rate subsidy of 3 per cent on ECU 1.5 billion of loans. However, at the time of going to press it was not known to what extent these figures might need to be adjusted to take account of Switzerland's non-participation in the EEA.

Northern Ireland will be entitled to benefit from this Fund, along with Greece, the Republic of Ireland, Portugal and the less-developed regions of Spain.

The Fund will be administered by the European Investment Bank (EIB), in consultation with the European Commission and an EFTA Financial Mechanism Committee. It will give priority to projects which place particular emphasis on the environment (including urban development), transport and education and training. It will finance projects carried out by both public authorities and public or private companies. In the case of projects proposed by private companies, special consideration will be given to applications from small and medium-sized firms.

## II.11 The parallel agreements

In addition to the main EEA Agreement, parallel agreements have been concluded between the Community and EFTA in the areas of Alpine transit, fish and agriculture.

### Alpine transit

The EC has concluded agreements with Austria and Switzerland on Alpine transit. These allow increased access to the Alpine passes for EC hauliers, whilst recognising these countries' concern with the protection of the Alpine environment.

There will be a limited increase in the number of EC trucks permitted across the Passes. In exchange, the EC has agreed to take steps to reduce pollution and to encourage the use of alternative means of transport. Switzerland has committed to build two new rail tunnels under the Alps, which will help to divert transit traffic off the roads.

The EC/Austria Transit Agreement entered into force on 1 January 1993. The EC/Switzerland Transit Agreement entered into force on 22 January 1993.

### Fish

Under agreements concluded with Norway, Iceland and Sweden, EFTA will give the EC greater access to its fishing opportunities.

The EC share of the total allowable catch for North Norway cod will be consolidated at 2.9 per cent, of which the UK will receive its traditional share of two-thirds. On top of this, when the EEA Agreement enters into force, some additional North Norway cod will also be made available for Spain, Portugal and Ireland.

For the first time since the cod wars of the 1970s, Iceland has agreed to give the EC limited access to her fishing grounds. A small quantity of redfish will be available. The precise allocation of this fish between EC member states has not yet been decided: but the UK is expected to benefit and is pressing hard to obtain a substantial share.

### Agriculture

Bilateral agreements between the EC and individual EFTA countries will introduce tariff and quota concessions by both sides on a range of agricultural products including beef, pork, wine, cheese, fruit, and vegetables. In addition to these reciprocal concessions, some further products of importance to the less developed EC regions will be allowed into EFTA markets at reduced tariffs. It was not known at the time of going to press whether the bilateral agricultural agreement with Switzerland would proceed, following Switzerland's decision to reject membership of the EEA.

## II.12 How will the EEA operate?

To ensure that the EEA Agreement is properly implemented and functions smoothly, there will be new EEA institutions and a new role for EFTA helping to shape relevant EC legislation.

### The EEA institutions

A number of new institutions will be set up to administer the EEA Agreement and to strengthen co-operation between the EC and EFTA. These are:

#### The EEA Council
The EEA Council will consist of ministers from EC and EFTA member states and members of the European Commission. It will provide political direction to the EEA, making its decisions by consensus of the two sides.

#### The EEA Joint Committee
Composed of officials from the Commission, the EC member states and the EFTA member states, the EEA Joint Committee will be the main EEA forum, charged with responsibility for the day-to-day operation of the Agreement. In particular, it will be responsible for:

- ensuring that all parties comply with the obligations of the Agreement;
- ensuring that the two areas adopt a common approach to implementation and interpretation of the Agreement;
- deciding which new EC measures should be extended to the EEA; and
- resolving disputes between the parties.

Decisions of the Joint Committee will be by mutual consent of both the EC and EFTA. In cases of unresolved dispute, there is provision for either party to take appropriate safeguard or rebalancing measures, which may be subject to arbitration, and in certain circumstances for parts of the Agreement to be suspended.

### The EFTA Surveillance Authority
The EFTA Surveillance Authority (ESA), to be set up by the EFTA states, will be responsible for ensuring that the Agreement is properly complied with within the EFTA countries. It will have very similar powers within EFTA to those which the European Commission enjoys within the EC.

The ESA will be based in Brussels. It will work very closely with the Commission to ensure that the two authorities maintain a common approach.

### The EFTA Court
The EFTA Court is to be set up by the EFTA countries. It will be competent to rule on:
- disputes between EFTA states on EEA matters;
- actions concerning the EFTA surveillance procedure (e.g. infraction proceedings brought by the ESA against an EFTA state for breach of the Agreement); and
- appeals against ESA decisions in the competition field.

### The EEA Joint Parliamentary Committee
Composed of members of the European Parliament (MEPs) and EFTA parliamentarians, the Joint Parliamentary Committee is intended to promote mutual understanding via dialogue and debate. It will not, however, enjoy any legislative powers, nor will it replace existing bilateral contacts between members of EC and EFTA parliaments.

### The EEA Consultative Committee
The Consultative Committee will consist of members of the Community's Economic and Social Committee (ESC) and the corresponding EFTA Consultative Committee. It will examine economic and social issues and promote increased co-operation in this area between the EC and EFTA.

## EFTA's role in EC decision-making
Once the Agreement is in force, the EFTA states will have the opportunity to influence new EC legislation in areas relevant to the EEA.

EFTA experts will be able to participate in the preliminary discussions of new EC proposals. Subsequently, the EFTA states will be fully consulted throughout the legislative process. In addition, the EFTA states will have the right to raise any concerns about relevant EC measures in the EEA Council or Joint Committee at any stage.

However, the EFTA states will not be able to vote on, veto or amend EC legislation. While the EFTA voice will be heard, the Community will, at the end of the day, take the final legislative decisions and will therefore retain full decision-making autonomy.

## II.13 How is the EEA different from membership of the Community?

There are a number of important differences between membership of the EEA and membership of the European Community. In summary, the main points are:

- the EEA is a free trade area, not a customs union. Border controls between the EC and the EFTA states will remain. EFTA will not take on the EC's Common Customs Tariff and will not participate in the Common Commercial Policy. EFTA countries will be free to set their own tariffs for third countries (subject of course to the requirements of relevant multilateral trade organisations such as GATT and OECD);
- EFTA will not participate in the Common Agricultural Policy (CAP) or the Common Fisheries Policy (CFP). Their own systems for agriculture and fisheries will remain unchanged;
- EFTA will not be bound by the Community's financial or fiscal policies. Thus, for example, there is no reference to membership of the Exchange Rate Mechanism (ERM), nor will EFTA be obliged to adopt VAT or to harmonise excise duties. Differences in local taxation policies will remain although these must not discriminate against goods from other EEA countries;
- EFTA will not contribute to the Community Budget (although they will contribute to EC framework and action programmes in which they participate) and neither will they be eligible for Community funding (for example, from the structural funds);
- EFTA will only have a limited role in determining the shape of EC legislation. They will be consulted on measures which are relevant to the EEA but, ultimately, they have no powers of vote or veto;
- EFTA will not be bound by the provisions of the Maastricht Treaty on European Union. For example, they will not participate in Economic and Monetary Union (EMU) or the Common Foreign and Security Policy (CFSP).

It is clear from this that the full provisions of the '*acquis communautaire*' go much further that those of the EEA Agreement, although this covers around 60 per cent of the text of the total 'acquis'. The whole range of EC provisions will only apply to the EFTA countries if and when they join the EC.

### Is the EEA only a short-term arrangement?

The December 1992 Edinburgh European Council agreed that negotiations will start in early 1993 with Austria, Sweden and Finland on their applications for full Community membership.

Negotiations with Norway are expected to commence later in the year. The Swiss government, which has also applied for EC membership, will need to take into account the implications of the EEA vote.

While some EFTA countries are likely to join the Community in due course, others will probably remain outside. The EEA Agreement will continue to apply to the relationship between the enlarged Community and those EFTA countries who do not join, unless both parties decide otherwise.

Even if the EEA were to prove a relatively short-term arrangement, it would still be worthwhile. It offers significant economic and practical benefits for both the EC and EFTA during the years preceding any EFTA accessions to the Community, which would not otherwise be available. The benefits of the single market to both businesses and consumers will apply throughout all 18 EEA countries well before any accession negotiations are complete: and will continue to do so as and when certain of the EFTA countries achieve Community membership.